Devotions

from Everyday Things

HORSE & FARM EDITION

Enjoy the Ride!

Tammy Chandler

Psalm 95:1

☺

Devotions
from Everyday Things
HORSE & FARM EDITION

by

Tammy Chandler

WordCrafts

Devotions from Everyday Things: Horse and Farm Edition
Copyright 2015
Tammy Chandler

Cover Photography by Grace Luke
Author Photo by Jonathan Chandler
Cover Design by David Warren

Published by WordCrafts Press
Tullahoma, TN 37388
www.wordcrafts.net

For my husband, John, who has loved sacrificially and supported me unconditionally through the years. I am blessed that you chose to ride this lifetime journey together.

I love you.

Contents

Foreword

When I was four years old, my Aunt Kay saddled up her Morgan horse, my cousin picked me up and set me in that big saddle and handed me the reins. As I rode around my aunt's backyard, a passion welled up within me—I love horses. I went home, began to collect horse figurines and décor and I dreamed of the day I would have my own horse. As a teenager, my parents moved to horse country, and I was able to work at a stable just down the road. Years went by and our daughter was born. She was saddled up on a pony at four years old, and the passion began for her. Thrilled to have someone in the family who wanted to ride, our horse journey began as she rode competitively and I became her glorified groom. Now six years into this, she owns her own horse who is her perfect match. After surviving a serious accident while breaking a colt two years ago, I thought my dreams of owning my own horse were gone for good, but this past December my husband surprised me with a Paso Fino, a beautiful light-gray gelding who connected with me over the summer and became my Christmas blessing.

This ride through horse and farm country is a journey, not a destination. We need good people to help us learn, grow and ride. Each day we can learn new things about the wonderful creation around us, and the Creator God who made it all possible. I am humbled and grateful that He saw fit to give me eyes that see the everyday lessons, and has allowed me to share those lessons with you. I look forward to exploring these trails with you, and I am praying for you. Enjoy the ride.

Preface

Devotions from Everyday Things: Horse & Farm Edition is a continuation of the *Devotions from Everyday Things* series. Each book is a devotional in which you will find spiritual truths illustrated in ordinary things. An uncomplicated approach toward helping you on your journey to finding deeper spiritual truths as you notice how God is at work in the world around you.

How to use this book: The devotions are simple, straightforward, quiet times with God. Each one contains a daily Scripture passage, an illustration connected with a horse, person or farm object, a Thought-provoker, and a Prayer starter. The Scripture passage will allow you to see where the connection to God's Word is; the illustration will help you to apply the principles of Scripture to something you can take with you throughout the day. The Thought-provoker is an opportunity to adjust your thoughts or actions to the principles learned from the devotion; it is also a Journal prompt if you prefer to write your thoughts. The prayer is a conversation starter about the topic of the devotion. It is an opportunity for you to thank God for what you are learning, and to ask Him for the strength you need to apply new Biblical principles to your heart and life. It is also a time for you to share your burdens and pour out your heart about personal struggles you are facing.

You can also join me at my blog site:
www.simplydevotions.wordpress.com.

You will find encouragement, updates, and more postings to help keep us all going in this adventure into deeper spiritual truths. It's time to be excited about being a Christian—we can enjoy the ride as we find the trail of faith in everyday things.

Thank you for joining me for this ride through horse and farm country in **Devotions from Everyday Things: Horse & Farm Edition**. I am so excited you have chosen this book, and I am praying for you to know God in a deeper, richer way because you have chosen this ride. Let's get started.

Horse & Farm Edition

Acknowledgements

To my Home Team—John, Jonathan, Jordan and Charity—thank you for allowing me to share bits and pieces of our lives with others as I write. To our extended family, thank you for your prayers as I write, and for sharing so many copies with your friends. It means the world to me that you have supported us on this journey to book number three.

To our Farm Family, the Jacksons—thank you for opening your farm and hearts to us on this journey. Thank you for your knowledge and your friendship. To my Hippology students and their families—what a wonderful ride as we learn more and more about horses together. Thank you for sharing your lives and your horses with me. To the Lays, Kriegs, Korsacks, Hayes, Tilleys, Stones, Shemwells, Danny and Jennifer, Marilyn and Charlie—we could not have done this without you all being a part of our lives. To those we have competed with and against, thank you for the challenge to become better riders and a better writer.

To our Lighthouse Family—I am so thankful for all of you who pray, support, encourage, and stand with me every step of the way.

To the publishing team at WordCrafts Press—thank you for believing in this book before a single word was written. Mike, Paula and the team—your encouragement, skills and prayers have made this possible—thank you.

To God be the glory, great things HE has done!

The Clydesdale

"Oh come, let us sing to the Lord! Let us shout joyfully to the
Rock of our salvation. Let us come before His presence with
thanksgiving; let us shout joyfully to Him with psalms. For the
Lord is the great God, And the great King above all gods."

Psalm 95:1-3 NKJV

I think he is my favorite draft horse. "Clyde," a huge
Clydesdale with a big white blaze, he is a picture of majestic
motion as he walks from the barn—to the photo site. He
stands big and tall as people walk up, pat him and stand next
to him as their picture is taken next to his great shoulder.
His owners understand that most people do not want to
experience his great strength and power, they just want their
picture taken beside him, and they are happy to allow others
that experience for a reasonable price.

I was not one of those photo people. I wanted more than
just to see his great size next to my short frame. I wanted
more than just a picture of a moment—I wanted to see
what this powerful draft horse could do. So, I went around
to the back of the barn, with permission, and waited. Soon,
the groom brought him to the barn. He stood patiently as
he was brushed, harnessed and yoked to the wagon. The
owner climbed up in the wagon and invited me, and the few
others who wanted, to experience the power as his great
horse pulled that wagon. Clyde leaned into his harness and

1

the big, heavy wooden wagon rolled forward. No grunts, no strain, just power and strength as Clyde pulled the wagon around the driveway and away from the barn.

Many people see God like photo people see Clyde. They want to be seen with him, but they do not want to climb aboard and experience His power and strength. They do not want to wait at the barn as He determines their journey. They want God to be contained to a moment—to a picture on the mantle, instead of a journey down the path of life as He pulls the load. I came away with a much greater appreciation of who Clyde is and how powerful and graceful he is in motion. Instead of just hoping to have a photo taken, I was able to see Clyde's majestic presence and ability.

Instead of being like those who want a photo moment with God as they give lip service to His greatness, those who climb aboard and experience His great power and grace learn the deep truths of trust, hope and confidence as they learn God is greater than just a moment. He desires a lifetime of pulling the load for us and showing us He can handle it.

Thought-provoker: Are you doing more than having your picture taken beside God in your spiritual walk? In what areas of your life are you experiencing His power and strength as you allow Him to carry the load?

Lord, thank You that You are strong enough to pull the load and I can trust You as You do it.

Amen.

Notes/Insights:

The Registration Papers

"In Him you also trusted, after you heard the word of truth, the gospel of your salvation; in whom also, having believed, you were sealed with the Holy Spirit of promise, who is the guarantee of our inheritance until the redemption of the purchased possession, to the praise of His glory."

Ephesians 1:13-14 NKJV

Adoption. That wonderful word that means a person, or a horse, becomes part of the family. It means all the legal rights, and responsibilities, for that person or animal are now bestowed on the family who chose him/her. Part of the horse adoption process includes the registration papers.

For horses with registration papers, their history has been written down. The previous breeder, owners, locations and even genetic testing are included on those papers. The new owner then signs and dates the papers, pays the transfer fee and the papers are then sealed with the new owner's information and ownership is officially transferred. Horse owners keep their registration papers somewhere special. Most I know have a folder or a file they can readily retrieve if there is ever a question about ownership. Old owners no longer have a claim on the horse—he/she belongs to a new owner and the registration papers are proof he/she belongs to a new family now.

The registration, or adoption, process is a beautiful picture of God's redemption of each of us. First of all, our history is written down—and it is not pretty. We were previously owned by the world, the flesh and the devil, and they abused us. Sin and wickedness were their tools; they wore us down and made our lives miserable. Until someone came along and revealed the truth to us, we didn't know any better. But then, a new owner came along. Jesus loved us so much; He paid the price of our adoption on the cross, through the grave and into resurrection power, so our papers are sealed with His blood. He paid the transfer fee we could not pay ourselves, and now we are His. He wrote our names in His own special place, the Lamb's Book of Life (Revelation 3 & 20) as His proof of adoption. All the legal rights and responsibilities of our adoption are complete, and our old owners have no power over us any longer. We are now members of God's family and when the old owners show up and try to make a claim, God shows them the seal of the Holy Spirit on our lives and tells them they have no right to bother us anymore. Today, our adoption process is complete and sealed and we are loved by the One who paid the price.

Thought-provoker: Do you truly live as an adopted child? Are you grateful for the price He paid and do you live so others know you are now a part of God's great family?

Lord, we are so blessed to be adopted and sealed members of Your family. Help us to live so others see we belong to You and are grateful for all You have done for us.

Amen.

Notes/Insights:

The Impaction

"Pursue peace with everyone, and holiness—without it no one will see the Lord. Make sure that no one falls short of the grace of God and that no root of bitterness springs up, causing trouble and by it, defiling many,"

Hebrews 12:14-15 HCSB

Impactions are scary. They develop inside the horse's gut over time, unnoticed at first, and then cause serious medical emergencies. Impactions keep the "bad stuff" from getting out and cause major pain throughout the system—even endangering the well-being of the horse.

If a horse owner knows an impaction is forming, if the horse gives some indication there is a problem, such as going off feed, drinking too much water, or not enough, acting listless—any sign that something is wrong—a good owner acts. The vet is called and a gut-check is done. Oil is given to loosen things up and allow them to pass. The emergency is averted because something was done about the impaction. But some impactions are silent. The horse keeps her normal demeanor, she eats, she sleeps; she shows no signs of anything abnormal, until it's too late. Depending on the severity of the blockage, surgery may even be necessary to try to save the horse.

Bitterness is a spiritual impaction. It usually starts as something small, unnoticed at first, but it continues to grow until it causes a spiritual emergency. Bitterness harbors the likes of hurt, malice, turmoil and hatred until the system has been poisoned and the person is overwhelmed. Bitterness keeps the bad stuff from getting out, and it keeps forgiveness from getting in to clean out the heart.

When we notice the first signs of bitterness—those little things like not desiring to spend time feeding in God's Word; or not wanting to pray; or becoming listless in our worship—we need a gut-check. We need to acknowledge the hurt others may have caused, but we cannot hold onto the revenge, anger, and other negative feelings that will clog our spiritual system. The release of bitterness will not come without the oil of forgiveness. If we act like nothing is wrong, if we ignore the warning signs that bitterness is taking root in our lives, it will continue to grow. It will continue to infect our spiritual well-being, and it will grow into a blockage we will not be able to keep hidden. Sometimes, it's a quiet time of prayer and fellowship that restores us; sometimes, it's a radical change. Regardless of what it takes, bitterness must go. Let the All-wise Owner and Father of your heart give you what you need to let the bitterness go today—let His loving forgiveness start flowing through you again and restore what has been blocked.

Thought-provoker: What bitterness is causing a spiritual impaction in your life today? Will you allow the Father to apply the oil of forgiveness and start you on your way to recovery and peace?

Lord, thank You for the oil of forgiveness. Today, please release the impact of bitterness in my life. Move me toward freedom and spiritual health.

Amen.

Notes/Insights:

Blondie

"Then they brought little children to Him, that He might touch them; but the disciples rebuked those who brought them. But when Jesus saw it, He was greatly displeased and said to them, 'Let the little children come to Me, and do not forbid them; for of such is the kingdom of God. Assuredly, I say to you, whoever does not receive the kingdom of God as a little child will by no means enter it.'"

Mark 10:13-15 NKJV

We are blessed to have wonderful horse friends. Our daughter has grown up with a natural love for horses. She sat on her first pony when she was just four years old. When she turned eight, our friends invited her to their barn to ride their horse. Blondie was a gentle palomino mare with big brown eyes and a big heart. Charity brushed her and got to know her for a little bit, then Kara saddled her up and hoisted Charity up into the saddle. As Kara led her around, Charity's eyes were bright and her smile lit up her entire face. Kara noticed Charity's enthusiasm, and she encouraged her to come and ride again. Charity did, and gradually Kara taught Charity the skills she needed to ride Blondie on her own. A bond formed between all three of them as Kara spent time teaching Charity and Charity learned to trust Blondie. Blondie understood Charity was young and inexperienced, and she made Charity learn the skills to ride, but she also protected Charity as they progressed to riding around the farm and eventually into the show ring.

10

Blondie gave Charity a chance—she gave a little girl who loved horses the confidence to ride into the arena and be judged by experienced riders—and win ribbons. Oh, yes, there were a few critics, but Blondie never seemed to hear them and she took that little girl to a high point award.

The critics in the arena were like the disciples in this story—they criticized and complained about a small girl being in the show ring, doing things that "big people" were meant to do. But Blondie and Kara were like those who brought the children to Jesus. They spent their time and effort to help her realize her love for horses was more than just a dream. Blondie gave our daughter the confidence to ride on and keep her love alive. Jesus gave those who carried the children to Him the same. He wanted them to know He saw their love for Him and those children, and He did not let anyone get in the way of His loving on those children that day. And He still waits with open arms for anyone to bring children to Him today. May we be the Blondies and Karas of this world and help children to see their dreams of being loved come true in the touch of Jesus.

Thought-provoker: Are you a critic, or are you the one who is bringing people to Jesus? Who are you loving on today?

Lord, thank You that You never turn us away. Thank You for those who have loved us and brought us to You and Your love.

Amen.

Notes/Insights:

Rat in the Barn

"Therefore let him who thinks he stands take heed lest he fall. No temptation has overtaken you except such as is common to man; but God is faithful, who will not allow you to be tempted beyond what you are able, but with the temptation will also make the way of escape, that you may be able to bear it."

1 Corinthians 10:12-13 NKJV

With two barn cats and two rat terriers, we should not have had a problem. We actually didn't think about it much because the cats and terriers were always around. We would see them out of the corner of our eyes as we were tacking up horses, or they would wander into the arena barn while we were riding. But, winter brings strange events and this particular winter brought very cold temperatures and lots of wind. We had the lights on in the barn, the terriers were around—they were actually curled up together on a small dog bed in the corner of the barn staying warm. Nobody thought it would happen, and then the rat stuck his ugly head out.

He wasn't in a dark corner of the barn, hiding in the shadows. No, he stuck his head out of a hole in the middle of the stall wall. And then he jumped. Right onto the arm of the trainer who was checking blankets and water buckets for the night. She hollered and flung the thing off and we all came running to see what had happened. Five of us were now on the hunt. The dogs were called from their bed and the pitchforks were picked up as we went from stall to stall looking for the insidious vermin who had the audacity to show himself under the bright lights of the barn.

Temptation is like a rat in the barn. We put up safeguards, we have accountability partners, and we think we have done what we should to protect ourselves from it. Then, when we least expect it, it rears its ugly head, not in the shadows, but as a full-fledged confrontation.

There will always be rats in the barn; temptations will always be just a hole in the wall away. We do well to not become complacent, to think our safeguards are enough to protect us. Today's passage tells us that God provides the way of escape. It is good to have safeguards—we didn't get rid of the cats or the terriers because a rat showed up—but in and of themselves they are not enough. When the rat sticks his head through the wall, let God track him down and let Him take care of it.

And just so everyone sleeps well tonight—the barn manager did get the rat. God will too. Let Him handle your temptation today.

Thought-provoker: What safeguards are in place, or do you need, to help protect you today? Where is your trust in God when it comes to temptations?

Lord, thank You that You have the power to defeat every rat in the barn of our hearts. Protect us from temptation today and help us depend on You for our escape.

Amen.

Notes/Insights:

Kathy

"For the entire law is fulfilled in one statement: Love your neighbor as yourself. But if you bite and devour one another, watch out, or you will be consumed by one another."

Galatians 5:14-15 HCSB

Competition has the potential to bring out the worst in individuals, but it also is an opportunity for the best to shine through. For those who think the ribbon or the placing is everything, that it does not matter who the competition is, they must be "crushed like a bug," or even if the belt buckle is more important than the relationships with those on the same journey, it is a hollow victory. But, for those who care about others, who understand that competition makes us all better individuals, who realize taking ourselves too seriously can have serious ramifications, competition becomes a building tool.

Kathy is one of those who uses competition as a tool. She has a beautiful paint horse named Red Man. The two of them work hard and when they enter the arena, there is a harmony of horse and rider that shines through. Red Man is a big, well conformed horse that does well in classes from the first halter class to the last trail class of the day. Kathy could be one of those who crushes the competition in attitude and demeanor, but she doesn't.

At one of the shows, our daughter did not have a horse to show in the halter class, and they needed more individuals to help fill the class. Kathy could have said any number of things—it's not my responsibility, I have already done a halter class today, or I don't have to help out—but that's not Kathy. She hooked a lead shank on big Red Man and motioned for Charity to come over to her. She put Red Man's number on Charity's back and led the two of them to the gate. She spoke to the judge, pointed Charity in the direction of the other geldings and off the two of them went to help out the others in the class.

Kathy's spirit of competition is a tool, not a weapon. She works hard and she does win, but not at the expense of the friendships she has made. And others respect her for it. When Kathy wins, it is because she deserved it, she and Red Man earned it, not because she stepped on someone else to get it. And to a small group of young girls learning about competition that day, Kathy was a good example. She helped when she could have walked away, and been justified in doing so. But it was more important to Kathy for those girls to see someone who was willing to set aside any kind of arrogance or competitive spirit and be willing to help them see the bigger picture—we all win when we work together. Only one person can receive the ribbon, but we all benefit from the relationships.

Thought-provoker: Where is your competitive spirit taking you?

Lord, thank You that relationships last a lot longer than placings or ribbons. Help us keep competition in the right perspective.

Amen.

Notes/Insights:

The Wheelbarrows

"But in a great house there are not only vessels of gold and silver, but also of wood and clay, some for honor and some for dishonor. Therefore if anyone cleanses himself from the latter, he will be a vessel for honor, sanctified and useful for the Master, prepared for every good work. Flee also youthful lusts; but pursue righteousness, faith, love, peace with those who call on the Lord out of a pure heart."

I Timothy 2:20-22 NKJV

They are not the prettiest pieces of equipment on the farm, and definitely not the biggest. They are simple things—great big buckets on wheels. But, we use them every day in the barn--wheelbarrows. We pile manure in one as we muck the stalls; we use another to carry hay or feed. We use wheelbarrows to carry saddles and tack from one barn to another. Sometimes, we even use them to transport younger children from one end of the barn to the other—at a bumpy speed as they giggle and bounce.

Some days I feel like a wheelbarrow—it seems I am getting piled high with lots of meaningless chores, I do not feel pretty, and I know I am not the biggest piece of equipment God is using in His Kingdom work. I wonder if I make a difference in the day-to-day chores I handle. In the great scheme of things, does the little bit of work I do in a small place on earth really matter? In the great house of God, what kind of vessel am I, really?

19

Then, I am reminded, God has all kinds of vessels—some are pretty, made of gold and silver and they attract others to the table the Lord has laid out for us. Others are wood and clay—those who are simple, down-to-earth, like the wheelbarrows, who have specific jobs to fulfill. They are not flashy, but they are faithful to serve. They are not dirty—they have been cleansed from dishonor by their faith in Christ as their Lord and Savior—and now they serve in whatever capacity He deems fit for them.

And yes, they do make a difference. Like the wheelbarrows, they carry the loads for others—burdens that are tough to bear alone. They carry the necessary nutrients of the Gospel—the hay and feed of the Word of God—to those who are lost and dying without a Savior. Still others carry the equipment we need to be able to ride safely through this life, as they teach the principles of Scripture. And, wheelbarrows get to do my favorite job on the farm—make children happy by giving them a sense of joy and freedom in the safety of God's farm, His Kingdom. Feeling like a wheelbarrow today? Good for you.

Thought-provoker: How do you feel about being a wheelbarrow for the Kingdom?

Lord, thank You for the wheelbarrows—those who have made a difference in our lives by carrying loads and helping us to find joy. Help us to be a wheelbarrow for someone today for Your glory.

Amen.

Notes/Insights:

Katie

"Behold, children are a heritage from the Lord, the fruit of the womb is a reward. Like arrows in the hand of a warrior, so are the children of one's youth."

Psalm 127:3-4 NKJV

It is a big responsibility when someone loans you a horse, but that is just what Penny did for our daughter. The horse Charity had been leasing had become a first-time mother, and nursing mothers do not willingly leave their little ones, so Charity did not have a horse to ride for that coming season. Penny heard about Charity's predicament and she offered to lease Katie to us. Katie is one of Penny's favorites—a tri-colored Paint horse with a gorgeously long tail and a steady trot. She offered Charity the next level in her competitive riding and our trainer said it would be a good fit for the season.

Penny allowed us to borrow Katie—we brought her to our barn, our trainer worked with her and Charity, and we took care of her. We provided her food, her veterinary care, farrier and show fees. Katie gave us the opportunity for Charity to continue to ride and show and Katie improved Charity's riding skills by being different from the horse Charity rode the season before. Penny gave Charity a wonderful gift—she trusted Charity to take care of Katie.

Children are a lot like a borrowed horse. Each one is one of His favorites, and He designed each one uniquely. He trusts those of us who are called parents with the responsibility to take care of the children He loans to us, and to make sure we rear them in a good way. Each child offers a new opportunity to improve our parenting skills, and He shares them with us for a time. He also does not expect us to do it alone. Just as our trainer helped us with Katie and gave Charity advice and wisdom as she worked with her, so we can seek out help from Godly mentors and gain the support of the church family as we rear our children.

And as with Katie, we always knew she belonged to Penny, and our children belong to their heavenly Father. He asks us to treat them as a heritage. A heritage is a gift of something that belongs to someone else, and something we are to pass on to the next generation. Children are a heritage—they belong to God and He entrusts them to us. Then we, in turn, prepare them to take over as Godly parents for the next generation.

We were so blessed by Penny's generosity and the gift of borrowing Katie. Each parent should see the blessing each child is, and the precious gift God has entrusted to our love and care. May we each do a great, Godly job of taking care of His precious, borrowed gifts today.

Thought-provoker: What kind of blessing is each of your children? How do they improve your parenting skills and make you trust your heavenly Father more?

Lord, thank You for the precious loan of our children. Help us to be Godly parents this day, and every day.

Amen.

Notes/Insights:

The Palomino

"Let no one despise your youth; instead, you should be an example to the believers in speech, in conduct, in love, in faith, in purity."

I Timothy 4:12 HCSB

"You can have him for free because I do not think he will amount to much." That is what the trainer told a friend of ours six years ago. She became the proud owner of a small, golden palomino gelding. She was a teenager at the time, and had seen this horse out in the field. She saw his potential and asked about him.

Romeo became her project and her passion. She worked with him day and night, sometimes sitting in the barn and telling him about her dreams for the both of them; other times training him patiently until daylight ran out. Each day, she taught him something new. Each day he responded to her training. Oh, there were times that he rebelled and refused, but she kept working with him. She focused on one skill at a time. Then, two skills put together, then three, then an entire pattern accomplished. Before long, he was able to change gaits with ease, follow trail patterns with leg pressure, cut and run for the barrels. He became an all-around horse in the Pinto world. His size was his advantage—he wasn't big and lanky, he was compact and able to change direction with grace and coordination. He learned to submit to his rider's cues and he gained confidence from their success, trusting his rider for each direction.

25

Romeo went to the world show. And he placed. This field pony, who was not supposed to amount to much, was in the ring of champions. Potential, passion, hard work, and heart had got him there. And they enjoyed every minute of it.

Each of us has had moments when we, or others, thought we would not amount to much. We were written off for being too young in our faith, or not-too-gifted. But God sees our potential. We become His project and his passion. As we yield to His cues, He teaches us spiritual skills we need. One step at a time, He leads us and soon, He builds patterns in our lives. We may be too young, or lack in this or that—our advantage comes when we submit to God's cues and change direction with grace and confidence that our Rider knows what He is doing.

Just like Romeo, we will one day stand at the world show. In heaven at the end of our lives, we will stand in the ring of champions. We will cast our crowns at His feet and enjoy every moment for we will be with the One who got us there.

Thought-provoker: Are you allowing God to use you to your best potential? What is keeping you from yielding to His passion and plans for your life today?

Lord, thank You that You see our potential when no one else does. Help each of us to yield to Your cues so we can enjoy the work You are doing in us.

Amen.

Notes/Insights:

Billy

"He must increase, but I must decrease."

John 3:30 NKJV

Billy was Charity's first professional trainer. He is a true cowboy, and he saw Charity's potential even at a young age. Billy watches each rider and after awhile he gives each one a nickname. Charity is affectionately known as "Smurf" to this day because Billy figured all the blue sports drinks she drank at horse shows would eventually turn her skin blue. The name stuck and she is known as Smurf in horse-riding circles. She is reminded each time someone uses her nickname of her friendship and connection with Billy.

Billy and his wife Katie rise early to take care of all the horses on their farm or in their stalls at a show. Billy rides each one, warms them up or works on training them; Katie lunges the young horses, bands or braids manes and she helps parents and riders as the show clothes go on and the hats and boots are cleaned and put on. Billy prepares his riders mentally as he talks through patterns and helps them shake off the nerves and channel their energy into the arena.

It is a lot of work. Billy and Katie invest their entire lives in their horse business, and not one of the buckles or trophies that their clients win ever go home to their farm. Their success is in the shadows of the spotlight on their clients. When they have done their jobs well, when they have spent all of their energy, someone else wins. Someone else receives the glory.

And Billy and Katie would not have it any other way. At one show, we tried to get Billy to go into the arena with the girls after a big win—he would not go. He wanted the girls to get the credit for the wins and how they rode their horses, even though everyone of us knew their wins were directly influenced by Billy's knowledge and skill. Katie is the same way—she stays in the background at her client's shows and she is the steady, calming influence when things get chaotic.

Each of us needs to be like Billy and Katie. We need to invest our lives, knowledge, skills and energy for the glory of another, Jesus. Our lives are supposed to be pointing others to Him. It does not matter what He asks of us—to rise early to pray, to spend time encouraging and working with others and seeing their potential, to be in the shadows as He receives the glory—we know the reason we are here on this earth is to give the glory to Him. He wins, and we win because we are a part of His plan. We shouldn't want it to be any other way.

Thought-provoker: Are you pointing others to Jesus or keeping the glory for yourself? How can you decrease today so that He increases in the lives of others?

Lord, thank You that it is worth every second that we live for You and give You the glory. Our efforts and energy mean the most when others see You and not us.

Amen.

Notes/Insights:

The Trailer Cleaner

"Such is the confidence that we have through Christ toward God. Not that we are sufficient in ourselves to claim anything as coming from us, but our sufficiency is from God."

2 Corinthians 3:4-5 ESV

Have horses; will travel. Most horse owners have at least one trailer to transport their horses to shows, trail heads, and vet visits. Trailers dot the landscapes of horse farms across the country. Some are small, pony-sized vehicles, others are so large they are pulled by tractor trailers.

But, trailers all have one thing in common—road dirt. If you haul your trailer anywhere, the trailer gets dirty. And although we may not have the fanciest trailers in the world, those of us who are fortunate enough to have them take care of them. This care includes washing and cleaning them.

When we first got our trailer, I tried using "normal" detergents to clean it. Regular household cleaners, car washing soap, dish detergent, window cleaner. None of them worked well. They would move the grime around a little bit, but none of them truly cleaned the fiber glass and made it shine. Then, a friend told us about the "purple stuff." Wow, what a difference! A little bit of the purple stuff sprayed on with water, and the grime just melted away. No more heavy scrubbing and scouring. Not only did it clean the outside of the trailer, but it worked on the inside too. Our trailer became like new again. The purple stuff did the job; all I had to do was spray it on and wipe it off.

31

When we try to live our lives in our own sufficiency, when we try to keep our spiritual lives clean with our own works and methods, it does not work. Life is grimy, and we get road-dirt on us as we travel through. We try to make things look good, but we usually wind up just moving the grime around a little bit instead of getting it off altogether. But, when we go to God and allow Him to make our lives shine, it makes all the difference. When we trust Him, give Him the glory, and realize there is nothing good in our lives outside of His grace and goodness to us, then the grime of life starts to melt away. We no longer have to scrub and scour the exterior and worry about how we look. God cleans the outside, gives us the beauty of a smile and He cleans the inside as well. He uses peace, love and joy, and the beauty shines through. Our lives are brand new because of His transformation in us (Romans 12:1, 2). He gets the credit for our clean hearts and lives. It's all Him—and He does it right.

Thought-provoker: Where do you need to hand over the rags to God and allow Him to clean your heart and life today?

Lord, thank You that You can truly clean and change a heart and life. Shine what needs to be cleaned in me today, and I will give You the credit.

Amen.

Notes/Insights:

The Arabian

"And when Saul had come to Jerusalem, he tried to join the disciples; but they were all afraid of him, and did not believe that he was a disciple. But Barnabas took him and brought him to the apostles. And he declared to them how he had seen the Lord on the road, and that He had spoken to him, and how he had preached boldly at Damascus in the name of Jesus."

Acts 9:26-28 NKJV

Some breeds have reputations, and Arabians are one of those breeds. They are called "hot bloods," "high-spirited," and even "difficult" by some horse people. The Arabian is built for endurance, has a perceptive temperament, is designed to live in harsh environments and has cat-like features. So I was surprised to learn one of the gentlest horses I know is an Arabian.

She was rescued by her present owners and they do not know a whole lot about her past. They know there must have been some training issues because she does not react well to loud noises and riding crops, but she does respond well to their teenager's soft voice and firm hand. She responds well as his ride, and he is able to ride her and do endurance racing with her. She can go the distance and she does not seem to tire no matter how long the race may be.

The Arabian reminds me of Barnabas in this story. We do not know much about him, except that he was from Cyprus, and he was rescued and redeemed by Jesus. He became a part of the family of new believers in the early Jerusalem church. There are moments in Scripture where he is challenging and high-spirited, but he also became a strong witness for the Lord. He surprised all the believers in Jerusalem by taking in Saul, whose name changed to Paul after Jesus saved him. He declared Paul's conversion and testimony when others were afraid of him. Barnabas did not react well to others' criticisms of God's work in Paul's life and he stood by Paul as his encourager in difficult days. Barnabas went the distance with Paul, even accompanying him on missionary journeys and evangelizing widespread regions as the church grew.

Under God's guidance, we also can be Arabians. We may be misunderstood by others, but under His hand, we can respond well to His leading and endure the race that is set before us. We can encourage others to accept God's working in their lives, and we can stand by those who are growing and sharing in the work of God's kingdom. We can go the distance and surprise those around us because God is holding the reins and showing us how to go.

Thought-provoker: Who are those in your life that need you to stand by them? Who needs your Arabian endurance and Barnabas tenacity today?

Lord, help us surprise everyone by the good ways we respond to You and Your guidance in our lives. Help us to encourage others to stand in their faith and help us go the distance because You know the course our lives are taking.

Amen.

Notes/Insights:

The Lunge Line

"No discipline seems enjoyable at the time, but painful. Later on, however, it yields the fruit of peace and righteousness to those who have been trained by it."

Hebrews 12:11 HCSB

Here we were again, going around in circles. I was holding the lunge line and he was on the other end, going around and around, being asked to change gaits—walk; canter; trot; stop; change direction; walk; trot; canter; stop anticipating my next request and just do what I asked, when I asked. Quit showing your bad behavior—rearing up is not going to get you what you want. Show me your respect; accept my authority; walk; trot; canter; trust me. Let's try that again. When will you learn that the lunge line helps you learn discipline and respect—it trains you to be a better horse? Was that a buck? Ok, go around some more and try it again.

If you train horses for any length of time, the above scenario has played out in the round pen, a warm up arena, or a riding area. You either start on the lunge line to help a young, or defiant, horse run out some energy and help them to be able to focus for riding, or you get off a horse that is having trouble responding correctly and you reinforce positive behaviors with the lunge line. In each case, you wind up going around in circles for awhile.

In our own lives, we sometimes find ourselves going around in circles. God knows the best circumstances and events to get our attention when we are young in our faith, defiant, or not responding correctly to His will, and He uses those circles on His lunge line to help us. We learn the disciplines of respect, obedience, submission. We learn to focus on His commands and not anticipate His next move—we learn to trust.

The lunge line is a tool, a good tool, to help horses. It is a training tool that keeps them grounded. Some horses refuse to learn on the lunge line. They get stubborn and angry, or refuse to work on the line. Then, stronger forms of discipline need to come into play. It is so much better for a horse to realize the lunge line is a tool focused on helping them overcome the bad behaviors, so they can focus on the good. We are the same. We should learn, when we find ourselves going around in circles with God, we need to stop, adjust our attitudes or behaviors, and submit to His will. The sooner we do, the sooner the circles stop and the ride of life moves forward again with Him in the saddle.

Thought-provoker: What discipline is God working in your life right now for good? Are you resisting, or submitting?

Lord, thank You for the disciplines You use in our lives to help us. When we want to resist, help us to choose to submit, so we can learn what You are asking of us.

Amen.

Notes/Insights:

The Hitching Post

"Be still, and know that I am God. I will be exalted among the nations, I will be exalted in the earth!"

Psalm 46:10 ESV

He stood there, totally calm, back leg cocked, hip tilted, head tilted to one side, eyes closed. The twenty-three year old, big, black walking horse had been out on the trail with his owner, and now that they were back, he was relaxing. He was still saddled and bridled; she had tossed the reins over the cross bar of the hitching post and told him to stay put for a moment. He didn't budge. He enjoyed the moments of peace, even as other horses were milling around as they came back from the trail. His owner had told him to be still, and it was not a problem for him.

The young white horse, had a harder time. He was antsy— pacing from side to side, as far as his lead rope would let him. He had to be tied to the hitching post. He did not want to stand still, and no amount of coaxing or restraint was going to change his mind. He was wide-eyed, nostrils flared, and every muscle was tense and anxious.

The difference between him and the big black one— experience. The young horse had not been tied up often, so when he was, he would get nervous. The older horse knew to relax, the time would come to be moving out on the trail again soon, and he was going to enjoy his down time. The white horse didn't know that was an option. So, his rider, understanding the situation, allowed him to stand there. She walked over and talked quietly to him, touched him gently, but made him stand there. Even when other horses were untied and moved on, she stayed there with him, waiting for him to calm down.

In life, we find ourselves at the hitching post. We have been on an adventure with God, stepped out in faith, done something amazing because He enabled us, and then He brings us back for a rest. King David understood this principle—rest is a good thing. It doesn't mean God will never use us again, or we did something wrong. Experience teaches us to relax, just like the older horse chose to trust his rider for the down time, close his eyes, and not be bothered by the circumstances around him. He focused on her direction to be still, no fighting, no restraints, just calm. We should do the same. And the white horse? He learned the hitching post was a good thing too, because his rider was patient with him as he learned. And God does the same for us too.

Thought-provoker: Do you stand at ease when God asks you to rest or do you resist? What needs to change so you can recharge?

Lord, thank You for times in our lives when You ask us to rest. Help us to be calm and enjoy those times just as much as we do being busy for You.

Amen.

Notes/Insights:

The Orphan

"There is no fear in love; instead, perfect love drives out fear, because fear involves punishment. So the one who fears has not reached perfection in love."

1 John 4:18 HCSB

A young, black and white paint gelding was in the stall when I arrived at the barn one morning. "His owner abandoned him—says he cannot afford him anymore. He's a little hard to handle, but you can work with him if you want to and see what happens." I walked over to the stall and he met me with fear-filled eyes. His ears were up and alert, and his body was tense.

"Easy, fella, I won't hurt you, just want to take a look at you." I tried to rub his forehead, he jerked his head up. I tried to touch his side, he would move away. A halter was out of the question. So, I just sat and talked to him that first day. I spent a week, just talking to him. Then, I went into his stall. Fear welled up in him again, but I just kept talking, moving slowly, and singing. Yes, singing. After a few more days, he would let me touch his side without flinching. We spent one day just getting used to the halter being in the stall. Then, the day came when he finally allowed me to put it over his ears without jerking away. Little by little, "Oreo" came to trust me. We spent time just walking around the pasture—Oreo would just follow me and I would make sure nothing hurt him. Eventually, he trusted enough to let me throw a leg over and sit on him. Then, came the saddle and bridle; the first visit with the farrier, and the first trailer trip. Oreo surprised everyone. I wrapped his legs, put on his halter and lead and led him out of the barn to get on the trailer. Everyone was prepared for a fight—trailers are scary places for horses until they get used to them. Oreo watched as I stepped onto the ramp, and without hesitation he followed me right on in. Trust had built a relationship, and that relationship led to no fear. And that was a time for celebration.

God is the relationship Master of this life. He knows how to drive out fear—love! God is love, so He knows exactly how to build trust in us. He keeps all of His promises; He continues to gently speak to us; He won't leave us when fear wells up inside; and He keeps us growing in our love for Him with things He does each day to prove we can depend on Him. I hope and pray that a day comes soon when God leads us into some great adventure—He asks us to trust Him with something scary—and we follow without hesitation. Just like Oreo, we can surprise those around us with our faith, and celebrate with a God like no other!

Thought-provoker: Are you building a relationship with God that is driving out your fear?

Lord, thank You that Your love is the cure for all my fears. I trust You today, knowing You are holy, loving and good.

Amen.

Notes/Insights:

Training Reins

"Examine me, O Lord, and prove me; try my reins and my heart."

Psalm 26:2 KJV

We are blessed to know several good horse trainers, and I enjoy going and watching them work. One of the tools each of them uses is training reins. Two, and sometimes four, long reins are attached to the bridle. Once the trainer is in the saddle, he/she uses cues to direct the horse to go in a certain direction. Each trainer reads the horse's reaction—flexibility, willingness, temperament. They watch for signs of improvement from the last training session and they feel how relaxed the horse is under saddle. Then they add a training rein to the mix. Training reins are used to change the horse's direction, sometimes a complete one hundred and eight degree turn, to teach the horse to yield. Some horses are so compliant, they make the turn with no resistance. Others show some resistance by pulling back on the rein, and the trainer has to exert a little more pressure on the rein to get the horse to change. And then there are "those" horses—the ones who would rather pull their heads up as high as it will go, back up twenty feet, rear, or run into fences rather than make the turn. They pull against the reins as hard as they can, and they resist making the change the trainer requires. These horses spend so much time resisting change, they don't get the rewards willingness and flexibility bring—a good pat, a break, and a release of pressure.

In our passage today, the writer asks the Lord to "try his reins." While the literal interpretation of reins is emotions and will—it does not harm the passage to think of this in horse terms. The writer is asking God to examine him and prove him—to give him a good training session and show him the signs of improvement and the areas of weakness where he still needs work. Then he requests, "try my reins." He asks God to climb into the saddle of his heart and life and decide what direction He wants to take. God is honored when we trust Him in this way—if we are willing to yield to His direction and submit to His training. As the Master Trainer, He does not take His job lightly or treat us unfairly. He will use only what is necessary to teach us to become what He wants. He will not ask for changes that will harm us, nor will He send us in the wrong direction.

Thought-provoker: Which kind of "horse" are you going to be? Are you willing to change, even if it is a completely different direction and trust that our Trainer knows what He is doing? Or, are you flat-out defiant about change, even to your own detriment?

Lord, thank You for being the Master Trainer who knows our hearts and just what we need to go in the right direction. Help us to trust You when You try our reins, when You ask us to change.

Amen.

Notes/Insights:

The Long Forelock

"You shall teach them diligently to your children, and shall talk of them when you sit in your house, and when you walk by the way, and when you lie down, and when you rise. You shall bind them as a sign on your hand, and they shall be as frontlets between your eyes. You shall write them on the doorposts of your house and on your gates"

Deuteronomy 6:7-9 ESV

Belle, a friend's Spotted Saddle Horse, has the longest, fullest, darkest forelock I have ever seen. It reaches almost to the tip of her nose. Her forelock is the envy of everyone in our saddle club, especially those of us whose horses are not blessed with the long flowing locks around the face.

When she eats, it's in her eyes; when she trail rides, it bobs up and down on her face in time with her feet. When she sleeps, it's still there. Belle cannot go anywhere nor do anything without her forelock being in the middle of her face. Belle also doesn't seem to mind. She loves when people stop and take a moment to enjoy her forelock, to run their fingers through it and spend a few minutes talking to her. Her gentle eyes peer out from under that forelock and show the gentleness and kindness that come from her good nature.

Belle's forelock is a lot like the frontlets of the Old Testament. Frontlets were decorative bands or ornaments worn on the forehead to remind students of the laws of God. No matter what they did, those frontlets bobbed on their forehead, or gently touched them between their eyes. They were there when they ate, slept, learned, played and lived.

God's Word is supposed to be like Belle's forelock or frontlets of old, for us today. It is supposed to be in front of our eyes, reminding us of how God wants us to live and love. No matter whether we are eating, sleeping, sitting or standing, we should be reminded of how we should live in grace. Instead of God's ways being a burden and something we try to hide, we should be wearing His grace and righteousness in such a way that others envy the life we have and want to do the same. The life of a Christ-follower is not boring or rule-ridden—it is a life of fulfillment and joy that should show on our faces every moment of every day. Just as Belle cannot go anywhere without her forelock being seen, so our lives should show His love. His love should be visible and His ways should be enhancing lives, not hindering them. We should rejoice when people notice God's love and character in our lives, and we should peer out from behind His grace and extend gentleness and kindness, just like Belle does.

Thought-provoker: What kind of forelock are you showing the world today?

Lord, help us to peer out from behind Your grace, love and righteousness and show others the life You want them to live—a life full of love, peace and joy.

Amen.

Notes/Insights:

Lucky

"Do not rebuke an older man but encourage him as you would a father, younger men as brothers, older women as mothers, younger women as sisters, in all purity,"

1 Timothy 5:1-2 ESV

Lucky has truly lived up to his name. He came to the farm as a temporary boarder, but he became a permanent figure—the farm mascot. At thirty-three years old, a former gaming horse with a broad chest and strong shoulders, his body has atrophied with time and age, but his personality remains strong and vibrant. His neck is kinked with arthritis, but he still holds his head up to look anyone in the eye and he can melt the hardest of hearts with his crooked grin and gentle gaze.

Lucky is also mischievous. More than once, he has been caught sneaking into the feed room, managing to break the seal on a feed bag with his old teeth, and eating his fill before being chased out. He picks up his pace if he thinks he can get away from getting caught for a bath and he prefers not to be stalled. He would rather wander around in the barn at night than be cooped up. The problem is, Lucky is such an elderly horse, and he has such a quirky personality, no one at the farm feels right about strongly disciplining him. He is "ancient" in horse years, and no one feels right rebuking him after he has lived so long and seen so much. Instead, he gets a gentle reprimand and most of the time that is followed with pats or treats.

Some would think this type of discipline would make Lucky unmanageable, spoiled, or difficult to handle, but it does not. Lucky has lived long enough to know when he has done wrong, and we know it does not take much to correct him. Just as the verse says today, we encourage him to do right—we do not have to rebuke him.

When we deal with the elderly, whether horse or human, we need to remember to encourage them, not rebuke them. Many times, loneliness, age, or forgetfulness have robbed our older friends and loved ones of their glory, happiness or joy. They do not need strong rebukes; they just need to be reminded that there are those of us who still look up to them, need their loving examples, and remember their achievements. Lucky may not be able to spin around barrels at break-neck speeds anymore, but we would not trade him for the world. How much more should we treasure the wisdom and memories of those who have lived longer? How much they deserve our respect. May we remember to honor them today.

Thought-provoker: Who is the "Lucky" in your life? What are ways you can show respect and encourage that special someone today?

Lord, thank You for the elders in our lives who are examples of Your goodness and faithfulness through the years. Help us to encourage them today and to be careful to honor them in our words and deeds.

Amen.

Notes/Insights:

The Tough Training Day

"A man's heart plans his way, But the Lord directs his steps."
Proverbs 16:9 NKJV

I had it all planned out. I was going to strip a few stalls and then I was going to ride.

Everything started out fine...until the third stall. This particular mare keeps a wet stall, and the shavings had done all they could to absorb the moisture. I pulled back the rubber mats and began scraping the floor clean. As I turned to start a new corner, I slipped--all the way to the floor. I had caught myself, and I wasn't hurt; just my hands and part of my jeans were now wet from the stall floor. I picked myself up, went to the tack stall for a towel and some sanitizer. I recovered reasonably and thought it would still be a good day to stick to the plan.

Chores were finally done and I was taking Oreo out to the riding area. As we walked, he stepped on the toe of my boot. He missed my foot, but I was already in mid-stride, so my foot pulled out of my boot and I started hopping around trying to get back to the boot because I didn't want prickers getting stuck in my sock. He got a little tense as I hopped. I calmed him, slipped back into my boot and we kept going. I then tried to put his bridle on at the gate. I had the reins draped between my arms as I put the crownpiece over his head, but he backed up and the reins fell between my legs. When I got the crownpiece on, he pulled back hard and the reins caught and flipped me over backwards. Again, I calmed him and got back on my feet. I stepped onto the folding chair we use as a mounting block and the chair broke. By this time, Oreo was apparently used to the calamities because he hardly budged as I fell through the chair. I did finally mount and we rode a few times around the arena. We were just falling into a rhythm when a few of the other riders decided to set up obstacles and run games practice. This proved too much for Oreo as we had worn through several layers of his patience already. I dismounted, disappointed, and we headed back to the barn. We would try another day.

The Lord directs our steps. I should have realized my need for flexibility instead of being insistent on sticking to the plan. I could have been more aware of the training opportunities these side-tracking events were and made better use of them instead of insisting on my own way. In life, yes, we can have a plan, but we need to remember to be open to His possibilities and not miss the opportunities.

Thought-provoker: Are you insistent on sticking to your plan? What possibilities can you see when you are allowing the Lord to direct your steps?

Lord, thank You that Your ways are higher than ours. Help us be open to Your possibilities today.

Amen.

Notes/Insights:

The Burrs

"But if you will not do so, behold, you have sinned against the Lord, and be sure your sin will find you out."

Numbers 32:23 ESV

There is a patch of sweet clover in the far corner of the pasture. It must be a really good patch, too, because the horses are willing to walk through and graze in between bramble bushes to get to it. We prefer that they not go to the clover patch on the far side of the pasture. It's not that we want to keep them from something they love; it's because the burrs from the bramble bushes get caught in their tails, their fur, even their forelocks.

One morning as we arrived at the barn, Dancer came to meet us. She normally greets us at the fence when we come, so this was nothing new. What was new was we knew where she had been all night. As she moseyed over to the fence, her forelock was sticking straight up—tangled and covered with burrs. Twenty-seven of them to be exact. We spent the good portion of half an hour with a comb and our fingers prying the burrs loose from her forelock. The time we could have been saddling up to go for a good long ride was sidetracked by the necessity of removing all of those burrs.

Though it was not a sin to go to sweet clover patch, the burrs are a lot like the consequences when we sin. They usually are impossible to hide—Dancer could not have hidden those burrs if she tried. They were right out on the front of her face for everyone to see. Everyone who looked at her knew where she had been.

And like we did, our heavenly Father gently, patiently, works through the consequences with us. As Dancer stood there and let us pick them out one by one, so our Father lovingly helps us, even after we have disobeyed time and again.

How much better would it be to obey, and even stay away from the temptations that lure us into unwanted consequences? How much better off would we be if we surrendered to God's plan and be able to enjoy a time of fellowship and worship with Him instead of another session of confession, guilt and forgiveness because of our carelessness? Holy living is not easy, but the benefits and blessings far outweigh the temporary so-called satisfaction of temptation. Remember the burrs and choose the trail ride instead.

Thought-provoker: Are we walking around with burrs in our forelocks from the choices we have made? If so, spend time in confession and forgiveness as you allow the Father to forgive you and get you back on the right track.

Lord, thank You for forgiveness, and that the consequences of our sin cannot be hidden. Help each of us to walk with You and stay away from temptations that lead to consequences. We are much better off with You than with anything the world has to offer.

Amen.

Notes/Insights:

Bullseye

"Then the Lord God said to the serpent: Because you have done this, you are cursed more than any livestock and more than any wild animal. You will move on your belly and eat dust all the days of your life. I will put hostility between you and the woman, and between your seed and her seed. He will strike your head, and you will strike his heel."

Genesis 3:14-16 HCSB

Bullseye is a high-spirited games horse who likes to have his space. He has been known to rear up and scare individuals on the ground around him, and while he runs a good barrel pattern, he can be a handful.

For the most part, I left him alone. When it was my turn to clean the barn, I would wait to clean his stall after he had gone out to pasture, or I would tie him in the cross ties while I cleaned on a rainy day. Every now and again I would rub his neck and talk to him for a few minutes, and he would always receive the attention, but then I would walk away and let him be.

On this particular day, however, he became my hero. I went into the barn in the morning and checked on the horses, and there in Bullseye's stall was a dead snake. Not just any snake, but a poisonous one. We figured it had come to the barn looking for a dry spot after all the rains that had swelled the creek and filled the pond. I do not know exactly what occurred, but I can tell you this, that snake's head was crushed. The rearing horse had put his front hooves to good use and that snake had not had a chance. I picked up the limp corpse of the snake with the stall rake and took it out to the burn pile. Then, Bullseye received lots of praise and an extra special treat from me. Our relationship changed that day and I never again saw him as a scary horse. He was the brave hero who had saved the barn from the snake.

Bullseye was a reminder that day of the battle of the ages at Calvary. Jesus crushed the head of the enemy, Satan, and gave each of us the opportunity to be saved from sin. Jesus was misunderstood by many as He walked this earth—they wanted a temporary king, He came to be the eternal Savior. They wanted to see signs and miracles—He wanted to save their souls. Many people today know of Him, they may even give Him some attention, but then they walk away. Today, allow Jesus to be your hero. Allow Him to make the barn of life safe for you, with a promise of eternity that will go beyond your wildest imagination. Let your relationship with Him be forever changed by accepting His offer of grace.

Thought-provoker: Is Jesus someone you know about or is He your eternal hero?

Lord, thank You for crushing the head of the enemy, Satan, and giving us the way to redemption through faith in You.

Amen.

Notes/Insights:

The Helmet

"Take the helmet of salvation, and the sword of the Spirit, which is God's word."

Ephesians 6:17 HCSB

I know a little bit about helmets. Through a series of unfortunate events in the late spring, my horse and I slid into a metal rail fence. I hit the fence panel head-on as we hit one panel and then slid into the one in front of us. My helmet did its job—it absorbed the blow and protected me from life-threatening injuries. I walked away with some scratches and bruises on my body and I did have a concussion, but I was able to walk out of the hospital, go home and rest, and still "be here" today. My helmet saved my life. Since then, I have noticed some things about helmets. First of all, helmets are not pretty. When I put my riding helmet on, I do not look like a fashion statement for the NY runways, but that helmet also serves a very specific purpose—protection. They are built as a rock with a cushion on the inside to protect the brain and skull. Helmets can also withstand a lot of pressure. New equine regulations have made sure helmets can dissipate pressure across the surface of the helmet and the material it is made of can absorb the shock of a sudden impact.

So, what does this have to do with being God-followers? Ephesians 6 tells us to put on the helmet of salvation. The world does not understand why we need a helmet; they think our helmets are unattractive, ugly, or even ridiculous. But, they are not in the race. They don't understand the fiery darts that are being thrown at us at neck-break speed. They don't understand the sudden impact of a faith crisis when life hits you head-on.

Our helmet serves a very specific purpose. It protects our minds from the massive impacts of grief, loss, death, sickness, spiritual attacks and family problems. Wearing the helmet of salvation doesn't mean we won't feel pain—I still had a physical concussion, but the helmet keeps us from being in a spiritual coma or becoming brain-dead in our faith (2 Timothy 1:7). It protects us and keeps us functioning as believers as we get back up, rest awhile, and then climb back in the saddle for another race.

The security of our salvation can withstand a lot of pressure, just as the helmet absorbs the pressure from impact. In fact, our heavenly helmet will not crack or "blow-out" when we have head-on impacts in life. The safety standards for our spiritual helmet are out-of-this-world specs that will withstand anything, anytime, anywhere in this world!

Just as I need a helmet when I am working with horses, we need our spiritual helmet to give us the protection we need each step of the way.

Thought-provoker: Are you wearing the helmet of salvation and allowing it to absorb the impacts of life?

Lord, thank You that our helmet is strong enough and specifically designed to sustain the pressures of this life and protect us for the life to come.

Amen.

Notes/Insights:

Harley

"Therefore, if anyone is in Christ, he is a new creation; old things have passed away, and look, new things have come. Everything is from God, who reconciled us to Himself through Christ and gave us the ministry of reconciliation."

2 Corinthians 5:17-18 HCSB

Harley is a perky paint horse with a blue eye, big reddish spots and lots of freckles on her coat. She was born and raised as a games horse, and she could rock the poles and burn up a barrel pattern in record times. A serious shoulder injury sidelined her from the games, and her owner, Melissa, knew putting her back into the games could result in permanent lameness. Being a compassionate and good owner, she retired Harley to a pasture in the backyard. At first, Harley loved the time off, but eventually she became restless. Being used to the speed, the shows, even the trailer trips, Harley was becoming despondent in the confines of the pasture, and Melissa knew she had to do something for Harley.

Rebecca Grace is a kind and gentle soul with a perkiness all her own and she is a perfect match for Harley. She knew about the injury, but she also knew she had a plan for Harley. Instead of returning her to the games, Rebecca Grace worked and trained Harley to become a ranch horse. She put a different saddle on her, gave her new tack and equipment and made things new for Harley. Horsemanship patterns became new skills for Harley to learn, and she picked them up well. She learned how to stand, spin, walk, run, ride like a ranch horse. Harley took well to the new training, and it wasn't long before she was ready for the show ring again. Instead of an injured games horse, she is now a winning ranch horse. Rebecca Grace and Harley have won ribbons and buckles, but the most important part—Harley's shoulder healed and she is not lame. Rebecca Grace's love for Harley and her purpose for her have made Harley into a new horse. Harley's perkiness returned, she enjoys being in the pasture again and there is no evidence of the limp or the injury she had before. She is a healthy ranch horse and she loves her new life.

Harley is a picture of what happens to believers. Our heavenly Father sees us, injured by sin and hurt by the world and its games, and He purchases us. He has a plan from the beginning of time for us (Ephesians 2:10) and He makes things new. He gives us a new name—His children. He gives us a new purpose—serving Him. He gives us His love and He watches over us as the injuries heal and we become the new creation He has deemed us to be. We become healthy in His love and we are restored. He gives us victories, but His most important goal for us is to be made new.

Thought-provoker: What has God done to heal you and make you new? Give Him glory for those things today.

Lord, thank You for making us new.

Amen.

Notes/Insights:

Smoke

"Be watchful, stand firm in the faith, act like men, be strong. Let all that you do be done in love."

I Corinthians 16:13 ESV

At nineteen years old, he should be living the retired life. Smoke is a robust games horse that has been strong and quick since he was a baby. He started out dark colored, but the years have lightened his coat to a flea-bitten gray. He loves to go to the shows and run. He is a calm and gentle horse, until he hits the chute, then his stride lengthens and his mane flies as he approaches each barrel, pole or flag bucket. He is the favorite ride of Tim, a reserved cowboy who opens up once you get to know him.

Both Tim and Smoke refuse to quit. Tim works hard all week long at his job, on his farm, and taking care of his family. He has been in his current career for as long as Smoke's been alive—a long time to stay in one line of work. When the weekend comes, Tim gets Smoke ready for the show. Sometimes, his family will join in the fun of giving the big horse his weekly bath, but sometimes Tim is on his own. He loads up the horses and the family, and they head to the show.

Tim could sit in the stands with other spectators, and he would be justified in doing so. After all, he has had a long hard week. But, instead, Tim is the president of the saddle club. He handles all the announcements, oversees the set up of the courses, and stays involved down in the arena to help and assist young riders and keep safety as a first priority. When it comes his turn to ride, his son or daughter brings his horse to the arena for him, he mounts and off they go. And even at nineteen years of age, Smoke is the one to beat. He runs hard and he does not give up.

Tim tried to retire Smoke at one point, but no matter what horse he tried, he came back to Smoke. The bond between the two—some women would call it love; most men prefer to call it success—keeps the two of them together. The two of them are just as determined today as they were when they started. They stand firm and they both act like men—they do not quit. Even when things are tough and the weeks are long; when the responsibilities pile up and the to-do list is never ending—they do not quit. They keep on giving and they stay strong. This is what real horses and real men do— they do not quit.

Thought-provoker: Where are you weary and need to strengthen your resolve today? Ask the Lord to give you the ability to not give up. Do not quit—you can stand firm.

Lord, thank You for the challenge to stand strong and act like men. Even in the difficult times, remind us that You are our strength and we can stand firm because of You.

Amen.

Notes/Insights:

The Sale

"Whereas you do not know what will happen tomorrow. For what
is your life?"

James 4:14a NKJV

It was time to finish the decision. The horse I had spent so
many hours with the past year; the one who no one could
touch when he first came to the farm; the one with whom
I had survived the accident and then persevered through
more training hours—was ready. He was ready to be trained
further in gaming—but those disciplines were not my
strengths. He needed someone who would allow him to be
what he was gifted to be—a gamer. He rode with his neck
high; a strong, long stride, and a power that was not
conducive to pleasure riding. He wanted to be able to run,
turn, go—live life with speed.

And so the phone call came. The rodeo family's daughter
had decided she wanted him and she called to arrange the
sale. We talked numbers and worked out the details—I said
what I was supposed to and in my heart, I knew it was the
right thing to do. I just wanted to hold on longer. I wanted
him to be mine for one more day—and another day after
that, and maybe another after that. But, reality had called
and the time was up and he was moving on.

Life is harsh sometimes. We think we have all the time in
the world to spend with those we call ours—our parents,
children, siblings, best friends. We spend hours with them,
working through their fears—or ours—deepening the

73

relationship and enjoying each other's company. We think things will always be a certain way, and then they are not. Career changes, college choices, illnesses and sometimes even death, cause drastic changes to happen quickly. We know our loved ones are ready, but we want to hold on just a moment longer. We want time to stop so we can stay in a moment—to wrap our arms around a beautiful present and just stay there. But then the phone call comes, the decision is made, and life keeps moving.

So, what are we to do? We can be miserable trying to clench the present and refuse the change, or we can get ready for the sale. I took Oreo out that next morning, and worked him one more time. He did great—at the gaming skills I knew how to teach him. I gave him a bath and he played with his tack bottles, just like he always had before. I brushed him down, and I worked on his spots until he shone in the sun. I took pictures of him, and then I buried my head in his shoulder and cried. I let all the emotions of the past several days to rush out the flood gates and down my cheeks. I prayed for him to be a safe ride for his new owner and thanked God for the majestic animal He had created him to be. I gave myself time to live in the moment, with the pain of separation, and the glory of accomplishment intermingled with the feelings of "what will I do next?" and "I know this is right." And he stood there, through it all. He was still my first horse—with all his quirks and talents—and he seemed to know we needed this time together. God had given us those last moments together—He knew we needed them, and I knew if I didn't take them, they would vanish like smoke and the time would be lost. I had learned my lesson—take the time to be in the present. Say what you need to say, even if the tears have to come with it. And then, let them move on. Let them be what and where God has called them to be. And let yourself be what He has called you to be too.

Thought-provoker: Is life harsh right now? Are you dealing with emotions and situations where you are desperately trying to hold on, or change? How are you handling it?

Lord, we are so prone to clench tightly to the ones we love, and yet, life keeps on moving. Help us to show our love and affection for those close to us, to show kindness to others, and allow us to live in the moment, and allow them, and ourselves, to be what You have called us to be, and then trust You. Let those times in our lives remind us that You are still holding on, and You don't let go of us, even when we can't hold any longer.

Amen.

Notes/Insights:

Moriah

"But God demonstrates His own love toward us, in that while we were still sinners, Christ died for us."

Romans 5:8 NKJV

She knew all about his past—his abandonment issues and his quirky personality. She knew he had come from a farm in Wisconsin and been moved around until he landed at the farm here in Tennessee, left by an owner who could not afford to keep him. She knew he had spooked, and she knew his love to run. She knew he was a rescue horse, and yet, she knew she wanted him. From the moment she set eyes on him in the barn and saw his big blue eye and black and white spots, she liked him. She saw his potential and she knew she wanted to get him.

And she worked for him. She and her mom worked out a job so she could earn the money to buy him. She could not wait for him to be hers and take him home to her farm. She had ideas about how to work and train him, and she was excited about the possibilities for this young horse who had had such a hard start in life.

Just a few months ago, she sent me pictures. She had named him "Hank" after one of the famous sires on his papers, and he had gone from being a little underweight colt to a beautiful, filled out horse—who loves to run and rope goats or cut cattle. He had found his purpose and his place—and the one who truly loved him, and he was happy and content.

Moriah did for Hank what Jesus does for each of us. He knows all about our pasts—our sin, shame, regrets, issues and tendencies to run. He knows how we have moved around from this place or that person to try to find meaning and purpose in our lives, only to be left lonely and abandoned by the world and its systems. He knows we are rescues—He reaches down and pulls us out of the mess we have made of our lives and gives us a new home and a new purpose.

And it cost Him dearly. He gave up all of Heaven and its glory to come to earth, and die for us on a cross. He opened the gates of Heaven with His own blood, and resurrected from the grave to be with us every moment we are here to lead and train us in the work and purpose He has for us to do. He knows He wants us. He wants us so badly He suffered the cross so He could have us for eternity—don't miss that. We are His forever love. Be with the One who truly loves you, and you will find you are happy and content, just like Moriah and Hank.

Thought-provoker: How does knowing Jesus wants you, just like we want our forever horses, change how you will live today? How you feel about yourself?

Lord, You are amazing. As pitiful as we are, You love us with a forever love. We are so undeserving, and so grateful.

Amen.

Notes/Insights:

The Moves

"Three times I pleaded with the Lord about this, that it should leave me. But he said to me, 'My grace is sufficient for you, for my power is made perfect in weakness.' Therefore I will boast all the more gladly of my weaknesses, so that the power of Christ may rest upon me."

2 Corinthians 12:8-9 ESV

I have a confession to make: I do not like change. I prefer the routine, the comfort, of being in one place, doing the same things and adhering to a schedule. Though God has created me to be organized and creative, I cannot find in the Bible where He is worried about my "comfort." Change is what helps us to grow, but somewhere along the way I got the idea that change was typically negative. Change requires work, but that does not mean change is bad. In fact, God designed change to be good for us. Each day is a change, seasons change, circumstances change, you get the idea.

Along our journey, our horses have lived on three different farms. Packing all of our stuff for each move was a big job, but it was also a time to clean out unnecessary tack, reorganize the trailer and the supplies, and get things back in an orderly system. Each move was an opportunity to get to know more good horse people, learn new things about horses, and to trust God had a plan. Each farm gave us the privilege to watch God create friendships for us and our children, and those friendships have lasted beyond the moves. Each new place gave us new experiences, new trails to explore and new routines to learn. Each one has been a blessing.

As we learn to embrace change, whether it is a simple change of attitude or a major life shift, we can find the blessings if we are willing to look. Paul said his weakness gave him the opportunity to boast of the power of Christ resting on him. My weakness—the resistance to change—gives God the opportunity to work mightily in my life as He shows me each move, each change, draws me into a deeper trust relationship with Him. Each change helps us to evaluate emotions, habits, and thought patterns to get our spiritual lives back into an orderly system of trust. We need those times that challenge us to clean out the heart trailer—to decide what baggage is worth tossing and what memories we choose to hold tightly.

And change is good. I keep reminding myself of that daily. As our children grow up, make decisions about schooling, their futures, and their callings. As my age ticks upward and I wonder what the future holds. As we watch our horses learn new skills and we become better riders—change is good.

Thought-provoker: What attitude should you have about change? Are you keeping things in the right perspective?

Lord, thank You for change, even though some of us do not like it. Help us to see change for what it is—the blessing and privilege to trust You more.

Amen.

Notes/Insights:

Hippology Class

"You therefore, my son, be strong in the grace that is in Christ Jesus. And the things that you have heard from me among many witnesses, commit these to faithful men who will be able to teach others also."

2 Timothy 2:1-2 NKJV

Long before some of my students had horses, they started coming to Hippology, Horse Studies class. We gathered as a group—quiet, shy girls who knew very little technical information about horses, but knew they loved the majestic animals with hearts full of love and respect. Young men who had been riding for some time, but needed to know more about care and training tools. Young ladies who had horses, but needed to learn about the musculature so they could better protect their horses from injuries. Some were passionate, confident; others were quiet and intuitive. Several years into the program, and how far we have come.

I believe I get to catch a glimpse of heaven when I hear the students share their knowledge with others. It does a teacher's heart good to know the time invested has been fruitful. Watching the excitement as parents come and tell me to keep the "secret" as they are stepping further on their journey into horse ownership and will be surprising their child with horse lessons or a horse of their own is a joy. Sitting with others as they have made the hard decision to allow a sick horse to be at peace, or lose a foal that was to be their next hope, is also heart-breaking. All of it, for me, is an opportunity to feel the heartbeat of God, even just for a moment.

God wants us to pass our knowledge of Him to others. It is a journey, not a destination, and we all venture in with different personalities. Some of the quiet ones talk of their love for Him and His love for them, and they win others with their loyalty and respect for God. Others learn the technical aspects, the deep doctrines, and they share those things with others who share their love of deep learning. Others share their passion for God's Word and His ways, others live lives in the spotlight with confidence and trust that surpass understanding. We rejoice with each other, and sometimes we sorrow together. This is His plan. We pass those gifts to others as we teach them what we know about God, and He keeps the heritage going from one generation to another.

I hope that one day when I am no longer teaching Hippology, one—or many more—of the ones who have been a part of my life in this way will continue the legacy of inviting horse-lovers of all ages to join them on this journey. More importantly, I hope those who have learned love for God from me will share that too.

Thought-provoker: What legacy are you leaving to those coming after you?

Lord, thank You for allowing us to be a part of the teaching/learning cycle. Help us to teach others about You in such a way that they want to pass it on.

Amen.

Notes/Insights:

Charlie

"As yet I am as strong this day as on the day that Moses sent me; just as my strength was then, so now is my strength for war, both for going out and for coming in. Now therefore, give me this mountain of which the Lord spoke in that day."

Joshua 14:11-12a NKJV

For forty years, he trained horses. He worked with the Big Licks—Tennessee Walking Horses that step high and show heartily. He was, and still is, competitive, but he is compassionate to his horses. He weathered the storms as other trainers were caught harming their horses, not following the rules. He continued to do right by his horses, even when it meant he wouldn't win the top honors. He stood for the right training methods and believed in the beauty of his horses, even when others tried to find ways to cheat to show. He was loved and respected in the Walking Horse circles.

He lived through the sorrow of losing his wife to a battle with cancer. He lost his best friend to age. He sits on the porch of the house he built, now living alone, but he has not stopped living. He is retired, but not tired. He watches as others ride in the arena in his back yard, and when he found out our daughter needed some help, he signed on. He became her trainer, instructor and encourager. He helped me learn the ways of riding the Walkers too, and he came to the shows to cheer us on. And after fifteen years, he climbed back into the saddle. One day when none of us could figure out how to get Dancer to gait at a full running walk, Charlie climbed aboard. We were surprised, he told us he had given up riding, but there he was making that mare look like a top-dollar show horse. He figured out the bit was not making enough contact in her mouth, and we changed to a medium port. He made sure she was going to do her job and do it well, and then he climbed down and put Charity back up on her horse.

Charlie is just as much of a horseman today as he was forty years ago—just like Caleb was just as much of a warrior. He had stood with Joshua and told the people to follow God's will and fulfill His promise, but they didn't. He walked through the desert with them for forty years. He lost friends, family, but he never lost his zeal to fight for the Lord. When the Israelites crossed over into the Promised Land, he asked for the mountain his feet had set upon forty years before. He helped the next generation prepare for battle. He was loved and respected. And God kept him strong, kept him going—just like Charlie. We need to remember we serve the same God Caleb did and we still have battles to win.

Thought-provoker: Are you loved and respected because you keep going for God? Are you standing strong and fighting the battles He still wants you to win?

Lord, thank You for the strength to keep going. Make us fit for battle no matter what age we are.

Amen.

Notes/Insights:

Markings

"But you are a chosen generation, a royal priesthood, a holy nation, His own special people, that you may proclaim the praises of Him who called you out of darkness into His marvelous light."

1 Peter 2:9 NKJV

One of the first things we teach in our Hippology, Horse Studies class is the markings and how to use them to differentiate between horses. Facial markings, leg markings, even body spots make it possible to tell horses apart. Even horses that look similar, like a group of gray Paso Finos in the pasture, have different markings that make it possible to tell one from another.

Some horses have big blazes on their faces, others have a small star, a snip or a stripe. Some horses have small markings on their legs, referred to as coronet bands, while others have white stockings all the way up their legs. Tobiano horses have big spots that can actually take the shape of certain objects. One horse we know has a heart on his side, another one has the outline of an Indian chief's headdress.

Each marking makes a horse unique. The markings give us the ability to tell them apart; their markings make them special. Dancer, our Tennessee Walking Horse, has a gorgeous blaze that lights up her dark brown, feminine face. Even in the late evening when we call her, we can see her blaze pop up out of the grass as she raises her head and heads for the barn. Without her blaze, she is a plain liver

89

chestnut horse. But with her blaze, she is our beauty and we can pick her out among any of the other horses.

God's people have their own special markings. No, they are not spots that come out on our skin and make it evident that we are believers. Instead, they are markings of traits that make us special. Galatians 5 gives us a list of some of the markings of believers: love, joy, peace, patience, gentleness, meekness, faith, self-control. These markings are a way for others to see that we are different. Today's passage gives other traits: chosen, priesthood, holy, special. These traits are to give us an identity that helps us to stand out in the darkness of this world. Why does God give us these markings? So we can proclaim His praises, and so the world can tell we are His. We live in His marvelous light, and with that we shine in the uniqueness of the traits He has given each of us to make a difference in the dark. Our markings make it easy for others to spot us. They also make us beautiful to Him, the One who paid the price to make us His own.

Thought-provoker: Are your markings, your characteristics as a Christian, showing or are you trying to hide them? Try living out the special traits you have as a child of God today. You may be surprised who notices.

Lord, thank You for the markings of Christian character that make us unique and different. Help us to live out those traits today for Your honor and glory.

Amen.

Notes/Insights:

The Rail Fence

"Consider it a great joy, my brothers, whenever you experience various trials, knowing that the testing of your faith produces endurance. But endurance must do its complete work, so that you may be mature and complete, lacking nothing. Now if any of you lacks wisdom, he should ask God, who gives to all generously and without criticizing, and it will be given to him."

James 1:2-5 HCSB

Little goats like to get into stuff. They jump on chairs and tables, they climb on farm equipment and they use their noses and small horns to pry stuff open. Things like the shed door where their feed is kept. And, yes, they are adorable as they do it, but it still can cause trials for the owners as they have to keep up with the little ones and make sure they do not cause damage to themselves or the farm.

The fence, however, keeps the large animals contained. These large animals could do serious harm to equipment, to feed rooms and to other animals. So, the fence does its job and keeps them out of the farmyard.

God uses fences in our lives. He uses spiritual barriers to keep away the trials and tribulations that would destroy His children. His angels battle for us in the unseen realms and Jesus Himself intercedes for us at the throne of the Father. When we reach Heaven, I hope He will show us the things He kept from our lives—things He knew would be too much for us to handle, so He took care of them for us.

But the fence is not a concrete wall. Sometimes, the little goats get through. Trials that will help us to trust Him more, things that upset the self-dependence and pride in our lives as they come in and knock over a few pieces of well-set spiritual furniture—our plans, routines, or expectations. As these little goats do their job of rearranging and prying stuff open in our hearts, we need to remember their work is allowed by the Creator of the fence. He uses them to help us look to Him, and to remind us that the bigger animals— the world, the devil and his demons—are contained from destroying us. God knows the difference between a little goat—a trial that will help us grow, and a devastating blow from the enemy. He took care of the enemy on the cross, and He keeps the fences strong and intact so we are protected. The little goats—round them up and realize they are blessings in disguise.

Thought-provoker: What "little goats" is God using in your life to help you grow? Are you mindful of the fences He uses to protect you from the bigger, destructive things?

Lord, thank You for the fences that protect us from the destructive things of this world and the devil. When the little goats get in, help us to remember that You use trials to grow us, not to destroy us, and only the ones You allow can get through. Help us thank You for the little goats, and the fences too!

Amen.

Notes/Insights:

The Trophy

"Being confident of this very thing, that he which hath begun a good work in you will perform it until the day of Jesus Christ."

Philippians 1:6 KJV

Standing in a line-up of twenty-nine horses was not exactly where I thought our horse journey would take me. My daughter, sure—she enjoyed the friendly competition, she knew the gaits and protocols, and she does well in the arena. But, me—I had always been a behind-the-scenes rider. When I was younger, I worked horses for a neighbor, the one who gave me free riding lessons in exchange for my barn and tack chore time. I can muck stalls with the best of them; clean a saddle in no time flat; and ride horses in the round pen and on the trails to work their muscles and specific skills. I can prep and shine a horse for the show ring without batting an eye, but show? No, I had no confidence in that arena.

So, how did I wind up in the line-up at the state show? I have a wonderful team of horse friends who refused to allow me to stay rail-side. It started with my daughter's nudging. Our farrier then said our horse was fit enough to take two sets of riders at the show. My daughter's trainer told me to ride for him one day and see what I could do. He started coaching me too. Our boarding family allowed me to ride one of their horses during the week so I could get some extra practice. My daughter's best friend talked me into buying a riding jacket at a consignment sale "just in case." Other horse moms cheered for me at local shows. I qualified. And now, here I was awaiting the results of a class at the state show.

The announcer started with tenth place. As he moved up the placings, my doubt settled in. I was not going to place this time. I was not good enough. Seventh and fifth places went to wonderful friends who had been on this journey with me. I cheered for them. I was almost ready to pull out of the line and go to the gate so I would not be in anyone's way leaving the arena, and then it happened....he called our number.

"Dancer, that's us!" slipped out of my mouth before I could stifle the surprise. The lady next to me broke into laughter as I gathered my reins and pushed Dancer forward to accept the trophy. It wasn't first place, or second, but it was a trophy. A trophy I carried into that circle of friends, trainer, farrier and family and passed it around for them to see and enjoy. After all, they had been the team God had used to do a good thing in me, to build my confidence and show me my fear had been replaced by hope and confidence.

Thought-provoker: Where in your life are you standing rail-side when you should be in the show arena?

Lord, thank You for the confidence You build in us through experiences and the love of friends and family. Help us share in the joy of stepping out for You.

Amen.

Notes/Insights:

The Cow Path

"You reveal the path of life to me; in Your presence is abundant joy; in Your right hand are eternal pleasures."

Psalm 16:11 HCSB

Horses are creatures of habit. They like to eat at certain times of the day, they prefer to be with their herd; and they do not like change. While trail riding one day on the back acres of the property, I noticed the horses were choosing to follow cow paths—small trails between trees and brush that the animals have worn down because of constant use. Even with riders on their backs to give the freedom to explore new trails, they kept to the same worn paths.

It sometimes takes a lot of coaxing and encouragement to get trail-set horses to try a new path. On this particular day, the horses were reluctant at first, but we were able to move them off the cow path to new territory. We persuaded them to do something new—to walk a path that we revealed, instead of the same old one they walked every day. We walked on through the woods and came to a level clearing. We stopped at the edge first to survey the land. We took a few moments to walk through the field to look for sink holes or big rocks—there were none. The horses enjoyed being able to stretch their strides, and pick up some speed, as we cantered across the new field. If they had insisted on the old paths, we would have been limited to trail walk speed because the cow paths had rocks, hills and tree limbs that made a quick stride difficult. But, here, in the new place, there was plenty of room to run, turn and stride out, and the horses were enjoying themselves. When they let the riders choose the path, we found a pleasant place to ride.

We are creatures of habit. We like our routines, our clan; and we do not like change. We choose to follow the cow paths, the ruts, of life, instead of allowing our rider, God, to choose our way. It takes a lot of coaxing and encouragement to persuade us to do something new. Sometimes, we have to go through the woods—taking one step at a time and not sure of what God is doing and where He is taking us. Then, He takes us into a clearing of blessing and abundant joy—a place where we can stretch our spiritual legs and enjoy His presence. He gives us time to do something different—to trust Him on a new path. Sometimes He chooses a change of job, or He moves us to a new location. Sometimes, He keeps us right where we are, but He asks us to do things differently and look for a new direction in our spiritual walk, ministry or family routines. Regardless, He asks us to be willing to trust Him as He cuts a new path, and makes changes in our lives, because He leads to pleasant places.

Thought-provoker: What new trail is God cutting in your life today? Are you willing, or do you prefer your old ruts?

Lord, thank You that we can trust You to cut new paths in our lives, and Your intention is for us to find the new, pleasant places You have for us. When the branches are thick and we cannot see far ahead, help us to know You know where we are going and it will be good.

Amen.

Notes/Insights:

The Barn Cat

"That ye put off concerning the former conversation the old man, which is corrupt according to the deceitful lusts; And be renewed in the spirit of your mind; And that ye put on the new man, which after God is created in righteousness and true holiness."

Ephesians 4:22-24 KJV

I understand that it is part of nature, and God created nature with order and design. Having said that, I was still mad at the cat. Just a few days prior, the tomcat had been on the prowl and he had been very aggressive toward the mama barn cat. She had kittens tucked away out of his reach, and he was mad. He flew across the barnyard and grabbed her by the scruff of the neck. They rolled over and over as teeth and claws flashed, growls and yelps were sputtering from each of them, and spit was flying as they tangled and hissed at one another. I broke it up. I have a hard time watching animals fight, and that day I was determined to separate the tomcat from the new mama. Yet, here she came, just a few days later, and walked right up to him and rubbed her head all over his neck. She acted like nothing had happened, and the two of them returned to their usual morning prowl around the barn. Today, I was mad at the mama cat. When I had broken up the tussle between her and the tomcat, I was angry with him for being aggressive toward a new mama cat. She was conserving her energy to take care of her little ones, and he had no right to attack her in that fashion. But now, she was going right back, acting like he was her best friend and the two of them sauntered off as if they had never fought.

How often are we like that with our sinful desires? They beat us up when we least expect it; they attack us from behind; they manhandle us when we are weak, tired, and discouraged, and they demand dominance and control of our lives. We fight back, and our gracious Heavenly Father breaks up the fight and gives us a breather. And yet, just a few days later, we go right back to our old ways as if nothing ever happened; there is no shame, no guilt, no embarrassment over what we had done, and we saunter off with our old desires like great friends.

What we need is a completely fresh start. We need to hate our sinful desires, be angry at them just as I was at that tomcat, and refuse to allow them to dominate us anymore.

Thought-provoker: Are you acting like the mama barn cat? Are you returning to sinful desires that are causing harm and pain and demanding dominance in your life? Is it time to ask the Heavenly Father to separate you from the tomcat of sin?

Lord, thank You that You do not allow us to remain defeated and attacked by sin. Give us the strength and the courage to stop going back and to start fresh with You.

Amen.

Notes/Insights:

The Barn Door

"'I know your works. Behold, I have set before you an open door, which no one is able to shut. I know that you have but little power, and yet you have kept my word and have not denied my name."

Revelation 3:8 HCSB

There is a humungous barn doorway at the barn where we board our horse. In the middle of the doorway, there is a big rock. The rock is big enough that the animals take notice of it when they are in the barn and walk around it when they go out. The doors are very hard to manage—it takes two people to close them, and it is still a challenging process. We only close them in the winter time to keep out bad weather. My daughter was curious about the rock in the doorway, so she asked one of the owners the other day why the rock was there. "Well, the barn doors rattle really badly in the winter winds, so the rock is there to keep them tightly closed. That way, the doors don't scare the horses."

The passage from today talks about a door being open that no one can shut. God opens the door, and He makes sure that no one gets in the way of His children being able to walk through those doors. He says these doors are opened for those who rely on Him, and do not deny His name. But, the rock got me thinking. Are there, then, doors that God shuts that we should stop trying to get through? When we pound on those doors and demand that they open—do we rattle others with our stubbornness and misplaced tenacity?

Jesus is our Rock. Does He sometimes put Himself squarely between us and a wrong opportunity to make sure we don't get through the wrong doorway? I believe in love, He does. In fact, I know He does. He tells us in Isaiah 55:8, "For my thoughts are not your thoughts, neither are your ways my ways, declares the Lord." Sometimes, the biggest doorways are open to the wide way that leads to destruction (Matthew 7:13-14), and Jesus wants us to find the narrow way that leads to a closer walk with Him instead. He blocks the wide door, holds it strongly shut, and waits patiently for us to find the opening He has provided.

I am glad Jesus is our Rock and that He sometimes holds doors shut that would lead to destruction in our lives. I am glad He is strong enough to hold those doors shut, and keep them shut, for our good. I am also glad that the doors He opens are held open with His strength, and not ours, and He has the ability to keep them open for our good.

Thought-provoker: What kind of door are you facing? Is Jesus strongly holding it open or shut? What are you doing with the open doors He is giving you?

Lord, thank You that the doors of life are opened, and shut, by Your strength, and that You love us so much You hold the right ones open.

Amen.

Notes/Insights:

Doodles

"They are to teach what is good, and so train the young women to love their husbands and children, to be self-controlled, pure, working at home, kind, and submissive to their own husbands, that the word of God may not be reviled."

Titus 2:3b-5 ESV

Doodles is a Nigerian dwarf goat. Her twin was still born and the timing of her birth meant that there were no other little goats on the farm. Without other little goats, there was no one to learn from or play with and we knew she needed both. Our daughter took on the project. She had learned about goats at a Veterinary Science Camp during the spring, and she wanted the opportunity to work with Doodles. The farm owner agreed, but she did tell us that Doodles would be going to a new home at some point.

Each morning, Charity would go play with Doodles. They played tag and chase; they would run and jump together. Charity would catch Doodles and let her lay on her lap as she got used to human touch. Doodles followed Charity around and they had a good time together as Charity taught Doodles how to be a baby goat. She taught her where the salt block was, where the treats were (in Charity's pocket), and how to ask for attention without using her stubby horns. She taught Doodles how to be a goat, but a goat with manners.

And it worked. A family came one day and fell in love with Doodles. We were a little sad to see Doodles go, but we knew she was ready to have her own home and family to love.

Mentors do the same with humans. We each come alongside of one who needs to learn her manners from a Biblical perspective, and desires to learn the ways of love, kindness and purity to be ready to have her own home and family to love. Each of us is in a place in life where we need a mentor, and we can be a mentor. We do this to help each other so the world sees that God's principles work, and they cannot revile (criticize) His Word, because we are His success story. We help younger ones to prepare to make their own marriages work by the grace of God, rear their children in the nurture and encouragement of the Lord, and keep their homes intact with good living. These things show the world that God's Word is true, and He is able to keep His promises and give good gifts to His children. This is where we as the church need to get to work. Instead of seeing a herd full of pushy, selfish, critical goats, let's lovingly mentor so the world sees a bunch of us with good manners and Godly grace.

Thought-provoker: Who are you mentoring today? Who are you allowing to mentor you?

Lord, thank You for the principles You laid out about mentors. We need each other so the world will see the miracles You can do in the homes of those who trust and serve You.

Amen.

Notes/Insights:

The Paint Pony

"According as he hath chosen us in him before the foundation of the world, that we should be holy and without blame before him in love: Having predestinated us unto the adoption of children by Jesus Christ to himself, according to the good pleasure of his will, To the praise of the glory of his grace, wherein he hath made us accepted in the beloved."

Ephesians 1:4-6 KJV

She really does not belong in a pasture with Tennessee Walking Horses. She is smaller in stature, a little more wound up than they are, and she is covered in spots. She is not always easy to catch, and she can be more stubborn than the gentle, older gelding and the steady mare. But, she is with them, nonetheless, and the transformation that happened has been amazing.

When the Walkers first arrived at the farm, she was in a different lot. She was mean, bossy and temperamental. She would jump fences. She kicked at other horses. She was kept up at night to give the other horses a break from her moods. Then, one day, the owners decided to put her out in the pasture with the "big horses." The older gelding accepted her, almost immediately, and allowed her to graze by him. The mare took a little longer, but she soon accepted the pony as well, and it did not take long for the three of them to form a herd. The two older horses started "training" the pony, and she responded well. She settled down, she acted less stubborn and she started learning her place in the herd. Even though she still does not look like the Walkers, she started acting more like them. She was accepted, and she knew it, and that made all the difference in her attitude and demeanor.

We are like that pony. Without Christ, we are stubborn, temperamental; we don't fit in and we don't know how to act. We are mean, bossy, sinful. Then, one day the Creator Himself transforms us. The day we accept His offer of rescue by faith, He moves us into a new place, with a new family. We are accepted by the beloved, and we start to learn new ways to think and behave. We settle down, we stop fighting so hard to fit in, and we let go of our stubbornness. We find our true place in His family, where we are loved and accepted, and that makes all the difference.

Thought-provoker: Are you still searching for love and acceptance, or have you found it in God's family? Even if we all do not look the same, we are His—do you believe it? Does it make a difference in you?

Lord, thank You for accepting us into Your family! Even when we don't look the same as everyone else, You have made us all one big family and we are so grateful. Help us to love others who are different from us, and help us to receive true acceptance from others.

Amen.

Notes/Insights:

The Empty Fence

"But sanctify the Lord God in your hearts: and be ready always to give an answer to every man that asketh you a reason of the hope that is in you with meekness and fear."

I Peter 3:15 KJV

It was a busy morning with lots of chores to do, and I was determined to get through them as quickly as possible so I could move on to some more enjoyable things. I was scooping up manure when I first noticed her. This particular mare did not come to the fence very often—she preferred to be far out in the pasture grazing to her heart's content, but today was different. She calmly stood at the fence, and when she saw me, she gently shook her head and whinnied to me. I looked up, a bit surprised when I recognized which horse it was, so I called to her. She whinnied again, so I told her to "hang on" and I'd be with her in a minute. She stood there, long after a minute had passed, and I still did not come. She whinnied again. I told her to just wait a little longer. Minutes ticked by as I continued to muck, and she continued to wait, and then she lost interest. What could have been an opportune moment to give her a good scratching and a chance to bond, was lost. She eventually walked off and made her way to the very back of the pasture again, and no amount of calling or coaxing would bring her back to that fence.

There are so many times people are like that horse in our lives. They have been distant, even stand-offish, and then something changes in them and they are hoping we will spend time with them, show an interest and give some attention. Instead, we are too busy scooping up manure—doing work that must be done, but not necessarily at that moment, and we sacrifice an opportunity for a relationship for menial tasks. We put off their requests for attention; we lose the opportunity to invest in their lives, spark their interest in God and answer their questions. We are too busy, and we think they will wait. But, they lose interest and, though our chores might be done, they have walked off to another place in life and no amount of coaxing will bring them back either.

Seize those moments! Learn to see when people around you need you. Put down your stall rake and take the time to go and give them attention while they are interested. Tell them of God and His love while you have the opportunity—life's manure can wait.

Thought-provoker: Who in your life is waiting for your attention? What are you going to do for them today? Who needs your time today?

Lord, thank You for relationships and those who want to spend time with us to learn more about You and Your love. Help us not to be so busy that we miss the opportunities to love on others today.

Amen.

Notes/Insights:

The Greedy Cat

"Let your conduct be without covetousness; be content with such things as you have. For He Himself has said, 'I will never leave you nor forsake you.'"

Hebrews 13:5 NKJV

All of the animals on the farm are well taken care of—including the barn cats. In addition to the rewards they get for hunting around the barn, we put out feed for them each day. One cat, Teddy, is quite spoiled by my daughter, and when we get to the barn each morning, he comes running to her for some love and attention. On some occasions, she will go in the feed room and bring him a handful of cat food to enjoy while she sits and strokes him. Teddy loves these moments of attention—and Mario gets jealous. Now, Mario is a growing kitten who started on solid foods just a few weeks ago. He still hangs out in the hay room with his mom, but he is venturing out into the world. He has his own feed bowl that he shares with Mama Gray and Tom, his parents, but there is always plenty of food for the three of them and he wants for nothing.

Which makes it quite interesting that Mario will eye Teddy and his handful of food. Mario saunters into the feed room when he hears the handful of feed being pulled out, and he sits and glares at Teddy as he eats. He swishes his tail and growls in low tones, hoping to intimidate Teddy. Teddy, of course, is not intimidated, but he does not appreciate the intrusion. Charity picks up Mario, carries him back to his feed dish in the hay area, sets him down and reminds him

116

that he has his own stock pile to eat. She goes back to spoil Teddy a little more, and here comes Mario again. He is not content with his food in his space; he covets Teddy's because it is not his and he desires confrontation to pounce on it.

We, as humans, act a lot like these interesting barn cats. God gives each of us special blessings—provision, protection, family, even a stockpile of food—and all we seem to want to do is eye someone else's blessings. We think we deserve what others have, and we will sit and growl about it, swish our attitudes like a tail, and hope to intimidate. We hope someone will abandon their blessings, so we can pounce on them. Like our daughter does with Mario, God gently reminds us of all the blessings He has already given us, and asks us to be grateful and content in our own space.

Thought-provoker: Who are you glaring at in your life today, wishing you had their blessings instead of enjoying your own? What are you going to do to change that today? Be grateful in your own space.

Lord, thank You for Your abundant blessings! Help us to stop looking at others and desiring what they have. Make us truly grateful for the space You have given us filled with so much.

Amen.

Notes/Insights:

The Percheron

"The Lord knows how to deliver the godly out of temptations and to reserve the unjust under punishment for the day of judgment."

2 Peter 2:9 NKJV

Standing at almost eighteen hands, with hooves as round as dinner plates and piercing brown eyes, he is quite intimidating. At one time a rescue, he now weighs close to sixteen hundred pounds and his broad gray nose and long flowing mane and tail give him a massive grace that is hard to describe. "Big Ed," as he is known around the barn is a percheron with a problem. As long as he is put in a big pasture or field with the fences far off; he is content. He grazes with the other horses, plays with the younger ones and runs with a graceful majesty from one end of the field to the other. His problem occurs if he is put in a small pasture, or worse, a paddock, where the fences are close and apparently irritating to Big Ed. In these small enclosures, he mows down the fences and puts himself in danger of being too close to the road or getting too far from the safety of the farm. When the fences are far off, the temptation to run them down is miniscule and Big Ed can control his behavior. But, when the fences are close up, he is overcome by the temptation to run through them and he puts himself in scary places without protection.

Sometimes, we have Big Ed's problem too. When temptations are "far off," and it doesn't seem like we are under attack, we are fine. We are content to the stay within the confines of our safe, spiritual pasture and enjoy the benefits of being with other believers. We are even willing to run the race of life with patience and grace. But, when we are placed in situations where the temptations are very real and "in our faces," we start mowing down the fences. We push down the limits and place ourselves outside the safety of the guidelines of God's Word.

So, what happens to Big Ed when he mows down the fence? Does his owner leave him on his own? Of course not. A very large halter and lead rope are grabbed from the barn and the chase ensues. Big Ed is too valuable to his owner to allow danger or an accident to harm him. Even in the middle of the night, if Big Ed is out, his owner is out looking for him. How much easier for both if Big Ed would just stay in the fences, resist the temptations and stay safe on the farm, no matter the space he has. How much better for us if we would do the same.

Thought-provoker: What fences of safety are you tempted to mow down in your life?

Lord, thank You for Big Ed's example. Help us to trust You, even when we are faced with very real temptations, and stay in the safe confines You have given to protect us and keep us from danger.

Amen.

Notes/Insights:

The Miniature Horse

"Then David said to the Philistine, 'You come to me with a sword, with a spear, and with a javelin. But I come to you in the name of the Lord of hosts, the God of the armies of Israel, whom you have defied. This day the Lord will deliver you into my hand, and I will strike you and take your head from you. And this day I will give the carcasses of the camp of the Philistines to the birds of the air and the wild beasts of the earth, that all the earth may know that there is a God in Israel."

I Samuel 17:45-46 NKJV

I have the pleasure of working with teenagers each week as we learn more about horse care and anatomy. One of the highlights each year is I get to see them show their horses at the county show. Two of the girls who show are Emma and Ellie. Their horses are unique, as they show miniature horses. Their horses cannot be ridden, as they only come up to Emma's and Ellie's waists, but they are beautiful examples of determination. Emma's horse is a sweet little horse that weasels her way into everyone's heart with her long bushy forelock and small horse attitude. She stands for halter classes, works in-hand trail patterns, and she jumps. Not just little jumps, either, she works hard to get over jumps that are as tall as she is. She prepares at home by practicing with Emma and the two of them prepare for the show arena with hours of determination and exercise.

Emma's little horse reminds me of David. Not the great king, but the shepherd boy, who wound up on the battlefield instead of the pasture field. He practiced being faithful on the back fields of their family farm. He was young and good-looking and it seems that people were drawn to him, just like Emma's horse. He heard someone mock God, and he was determined to make a difference. He saw the jump was high and the obstacle was not easy, but he was determined to fight the one who dared to mock his Lord.

Most of us know the story; Goliath mocked and called David names. David remained undeterred as he put a rock in the sling and ran toward that giant. A great victory was won that day because one young, inexperienced boy refused to allow a mockery of God to go unchallenged. The time he spent preparing in the back fields had prepared him for the battlefield. Just as Emma's horse does not back down from a jump, David did not back down from a challenge. We need to have more small horse attitude and be determined. The giants will fall, and we will clear the obstacles one at a time as God gives us the victory.

Thought-provoker: Where are you in your preparation and determination spiritually?

Lord, thank You for preparing us for the battles. May we not back down from the obstacles that give us the opportunity to show Your glory to others.

Amen.

Notes/Insights:

Rocky

"Don't neglect to do what is good and to share, for God is pleased with such sacrifices. Obey your leaders and submit to them, for they keep watch over your souls as those who will give an account, so that they can do this with joy and not with grief, for that would be unprofitable for you."

Hebrews 13:16-17 HCSB

Rocky is a Great Pyrenees and collie mix, and he is the protector of the farm. No one gets through the gate unless Rocky greets them and one of the owners gives permission. Rocky also watches over the farm animals and protects them. Rocky has gone after foxes, possums, and even skunks that have threatened the welfare of the livestock in his care. Rocky knows the owners are counting on him to keep the farm safe from vermin, thieves and scavengers.

One day recently I heard a commotion outside the barn. Rocky was barking fiercely, which is not common for him. I went to check and just before I got to the door, I heard him yelp. Now very concerned, I ran to the door just in time to see Rocky rubbing his face in the dirt—in front of a skunk. The smell reached me just as I saw the scene. Undeterred, Rocky again faced off with the skunk, but this time he chased it into the woods. A few moments later, the battle was over and the skunk was no longer going to threaten the chickens and other small farm animals. He came back to the barn, stench and all, and laid down outside the door to protect the farm, ready once again for whatever came. We praised him for his good work, and we even went and petted him, in spite of the smell, because he had protected us and the animals, and we knew he would do it again when needed.

Rocky reminds me of the good, wise men I know who are pastors. They do not own the "herd," but they protect and stand guard, knowing God holds them accountable. They welcome new converts into the family and they are loyal to their heavenly Father. They are willing to put themselves in harm's way to protect the flock.

And sometimes their job stinks. They are on the front lines of the spiritual battle and the enemy is merciless. Pastors fight the battles no one would choose for themselves, and sometimes they are sprayed with insults, hurt by people with bad intentions or rebellious hearts, or wearied by the pressure. Yet they are undeterred and continue to fight until the battles are over. These men deserve our respect, our goodness and our generosity. We need to appreciate the work they do, the battles they fight and we need to praise them and lift them in prayer.

Thought-provoker: Do you lift your pastor in prayer and praise? Do you truly appreciate him for who he is and the battles he fights? Bless your pastor in some way today.

Lord, thank You for our pastors! Remind us daily to lift them up as they fight the battles.

Amen.

Notes/Insights:

The Farm Family

"And He personally gave some to be apostles, some prophets, some evangelists, some pastors and teachers, for the training of the saints in the work of ministry, to build up the body of Christ."

Ephesians 4:11-12 HCSB

For those of you who have read the other Devotions from Everyday Things books, you have probably noticed that our sons have not been mentioned much in this one. Our boys do not share their mother's love of farm and horses, but every once in a while they will come out to the farm. Rodney and Marsha are wonderful examples of accepting people for the gifts and talents they have and they welcome our boys—with four wheelers, tractors, and good food. Our daughter and I prefer to ride the four-footed creatures; the boys and my husband enjoy the four-wheeled kind. They also enjoy spending time outdoors, in the woods, and moving stuff with tractors. Rodney and Marsha realize our boys do not have the same inclinations as our daughter does, but that does not matter to them—they allow our young men to have fun with the motorized horse power, get their hands dirty with farm work, and they do not expect them to be something they are not, or pretend to like something they are not interested in doing.

God appreciates diversity. He knew if He gave everyone the same gifts, only one kind of job would get done. If everyone were an evangelist, we would have lots of new converts with little knowledge or guidance. If everyone were a teacher, we would have many illustrations, but few to apply them. The family would be incomplete, dull and useless in all areas but one. God knew this, and in His wisdom, He gave us different gifts and talents. He knew some people would need to be the riders, the trainers and the trail guides, while others would need to know how to take care of the horses, repair farm equipment and move piles of manure. Each job is just as important as another—each farm family is incomplete without them all working together.

We are so blessed by our farm family. We need to be reminded that different is ok, and we can accept each other with the gifts and talents that make our family complete. We need to know we each have a place, and a job to do that is only ours to fill. Purpose, given by our wise, heavenly Father, gives our lives meaning. We cannot find that meaning if we are doing someone else's job, and we will frustrate others around us if we do not accept them as they are too.

Thought-provoker: Do you accept your gifts and talents as your fit in God's family, or do you wish you were something different? Are you willing to accept others in the way God designed them or are you trying to change them?

Lord, thank You for the reminder to accept ourselves in Your plan and design and to not try to be, or make someone else be, something we are not.

Amen.

Notes/Insights:

The Hay Loft

"Four things on earth are small, yet they are extremely wise: the ants are not a strong people, yet they store up their food in the summer."

Proverbs 30:24-25 HCSB

Summertime is a time of busy activity. There are always chores to be done, hay fields to tend, horses to ride, and on and on the list goes. Wintertime is a time of rest. Yes, there are still chores to do, but the list, and the daylight hours are shorter, so there is time to sit and reflect. Time to rest, relax and remember to trust our God as He provides all we need. If we have prepared, if we looked ahead and realized some of the lush greenness around our hearts needed to be stored up and remembered for a later time, we then have what we need to get through those dry times.

Hay is on every horse owner's mind at the end of summer. Whether we cut our own hay, or purchase it from a farm, questions run through our minds. Did we put up enough hay for the winter? How much will they eat? Will I be able to get more during the winter if I need it?

Without drought conditions, hay is plentiful in summer. It comes in the form of field grass, and the horses love to spend a lazy afternoon grazing on the lush greenness around them. Horse owners allow the horses to graze in certain fields, but other fields are left to grow so they can be cut for hay. They watch the fields, watch the weather and when the time is right they cut the grass. They let it sit for a few days to dry out, and then they bale and collect the hay. It is then loaded on a trailer and taken to the loft for dry, clean storage until they need it.

The hay loft is like the heart of the believer. It is the place to store up memories of the summer blessings—when times are good, life is full of activity, and God's provision is more than plentiful. We tuck those summer blessings away in our minds, so when the winter comes, those blessings feed our souls and get us through. Winter—those times of trials, or testing; doubts or questions, when we find it hard to find spiritual nourishment, are also the times when we remember. The promises of renewal are strengthened and we do not need to panic during the cold and grassless seasons that come with sorrow. We feed from the stored up treasures in the heart, rest and trust during the winter, and remember that spring comes again soon, for our God is always faithful.

Thought-provoker: What season are you in right now? Are you remembering your blessings? Are you resting and trusting?

Lord, thank You for the hayloft of the heart to store up treasured memories that remind us of Your faithfulness when all we can see is winter. Help us remember You do all things well, and the winter won't last forever.

Amen.

Notes/Insights:

Mama Gray

"For we do not wrestle against flesh and blood, but against principalities, against powers, against the rulers of the darkness of this age, against spiritual hosts of wickedness in the heavenly places. Therefore take up the whole armor of God, that you may be able to withstand in the evil day, and having done all, to stand."

Ephesians 6:12-13 NKJV

She is a small, but very passionate, mama cat. She is not strong, but when the farm dog got too close to her last kitten, she put up a good fight. She did not attack the dog head-on; she used her teeth and claws on his under belly and back legs. She attacked from underneath, and she moved quickly and attacked sharply. Her size and skill were her advantages. She was tenacious and determined to protect her kitten. And she did. She pulled the dog's attention away from the kitten just long enough for the kitten to run to safety under the barn wall. Mama Gray did not stay to fight longer than she needed, as soon as her kitten was safe she also ran to the safety of the barn, but she made sure that dog knew to leave her kitten alone.

We have enemies in this world, but they are not other humans. They are the guard dogs of the powers and systems of this world, and they are big. Spiritually, we are small compared to them, but God has given us a unique fighting style. He has given us an armor for protection, and we fight from underneath. The passage says the powers of wickedness are in the heavenly places. Taking the powers of this world head-on, we will not win. But when we use the weapons God has given us, the weapons of prayer, and His Word, and attack the enemy from underneath—from our earthly position—we can win. Our weapons are sharp and quick (Hebrews 4:12). We need to use our position to our advantage—we are soldiers who fight for the heavenly kingdom, and we have been assured victory by our Commander (I Corinthians 15:57).

Why did Mama Gray attack the farm dog? To protect her kitten. Why should we attack the systems of this world? To protect our children, both the physical and spiritual ones. We must be determined and tenacious, just as Mama Gray would not stop fighting until her kitten was safe, we cannot let up until we know the next generation is armed and ready to fight the battle for themselves. We need to continue to take on the guard dogs of this world, using the weapons and skill God has given us to let them know we are a force to be reckoned with because we come in the name of the Lord.

Thought-provoker: Are you fighting the spiritual battle for your children? Are you fighting with the weapons God has provided and are you determined to keep fighting?

Lord, thank You for the "Mama Grays" in each of our lives that fight for us spiritually on their knees and with Your Word. Help us to be a Mama Gray for someone today.

Amen.

Notes/Insights:

The Feeder

"When the scribes of the Pharisees saw that He was eating with sinners and tax collectors, they asked His disciples, 'Why does He eat with tax collectors and sinners?' When Jesus heard this, He told them, 'Those who are well don't need a doctor, but the sick do need one. I didn't come to call the righteous, but sinners.'"

Mark 2:16-17 HCSB

There was a commotion in the barn at the feeder, so I went to investigate. There, in the common feeding area, were two horses and two goats. The one horse was indignant that the goats had invaded her space, and she was tossing her head, knocking the feeders and chasing the goats. She succeeded in chasing the goats out of the barn, but as she turned back to enjoy the hay, she was met by the second horse. An older, buckskin mare, respected by the entire herd, was standing between the first horse and the hay. She laid her ears back, and lunged at the first horse. The unexpected aggression caused the first horse to spin on her heels and run out of the barn with her tail tucked. The older horse then went and gently corralled the goats and brought them back to the feeder. She stood there with them, all three picking hay out of the feeder and enjoying a meal together.

In life, we choose which horse we are like. When goats, those who do not believe the Gospel, want to come and join us for a meal, how do we respond? When they are interested in visiting our churches, or want to spend time seeing us in action, or maybe they want to ask us questions that take time to answer—which one are we like? Do we become indignant that goats want to eat with us? Do we cause ruckuses and chase them off? Or, are we like the older mare who understood that sharing a meal with the goats was the right thing to do. Are we willing to challenge others to make sure the goats get the opportunity to come and dine with us?

The Pharisees were indignant that Christ ate with sinners. After all, if He claimed to be God (which He did, and yes, He was) then why would He stoop to that level? It was as if Jesus were reaching to the lowest of the low in their religious system. Why would He bother? And yet He did— He stooped to eat with you and me. When we accepted His offer, He moved us to His table and gave us His name. If, for no other reason than a heart full of gratefulness, let the goats come eat with us. We are all His creation and maybe, just maybe, the goats will realize they belong with the horses and accept His offer too.

Thought-provoker: Which horse are you choosing to be like? What are you doing to encourage unbelievers to come and eat with you at your heavenly Father's table?

Lord, thank You that there is room for all of us at Your table. Help us encourage others to come and join us.

Amen.

Notes/Insights:

The Forever Horse

"Then I saw heaven opened, and there was a white horse. Its rider is called Faithful and True, and He judges and makes war in righteousness...He wore a robe stained with blood, and His name is the Word of God. The armies that were in heaven followed Him on white horses, wearing pure white linen."

Revelation 19:11, 13-14 HCSB

Each true horse lover longs for a forever horse—that horse they will bond with and keep for as long as they live. For some, the search goes on for a lifetime. They have horses, but they never seem to live up to that expectation in the back of their mind. A few special individuals do find that horse that they love and spend a lifetime riding and loving, but for most, it is a dream.

Regardless of whether we find the forever horse here—there is hope. For those who know Christ as Lord and Savior, one day we will each ride a white horse. White horses are a symbol of victory, and we will be dressed in pure white linen as we ride. White horses are the rarest—the genetic line up that must occur to get a truly white horse is a very rare event. Yet, heaven will be filled with them and each one of us will ride one of these majestic creatures. And what a ride that will be. We will follow Christ as He is revealed as King of Kings and Lord of Lords. Revelation goes on in the following chapters to describe His rule and reign (Revelation 19-21), and we join Him as His bride on this ride. For those who were disappointed by others in life, for those who were persecuted, troubled and tested, for

140

those who were torn down by illness or those who were wracked with regret—the end is a victory ride. What makes that ride possible? Faith in the rider who is called Faithful and True. It does not matter when you turned to Him, it matters that you surrendered to the belief that the work He did on the cross was for you and it was enough. He paid the price for your sin and you accepted His gift (Romans 6:23). If you have not, now is the time (2 Corinthians 6:3). For all of us who have, there is a forever horse in heaven to ride behind the greatest rider of all time—He who is called Faithful and True, Jesus Christ Himself!

Thought-provoker: Are you ready for the ride of a lifetime on your forever horse? Have you bowed the knee to Jesus as Savior and Lord? Are you living in that reality today?

Lord, thank You that You are the greatest rider of all time— the One called Faithful and True. Thank You for the promise that each of us will ride a forever horse, falling in line as You lead us to the victory of a lifetime. Help us live in the reality of Your lordship today.

Amen.

Notes/Insights:

The Barn Rules

"He said to him, 'Love the Lord your God with all your heart, with all your soul, and with all your mind. This is the greatest and most important command. The second is like it: Love your neighbor as yourself. All the Law and the Prophets depend on these two commands.'"

Matthew 22:37-39 HCSB

Whether we like it or not, every barn has rules. Some rules are simple—keep the hallways clear and safe; keep your tack in your designated area. Others are a little more complex—respect others; respect the management. What exactly do those rules entail? We understand the simple ones, and we know the expectations that come with them. If I do not keep my tack picked up and out of the way, someone else may move it, or the management may put it up for me, and I will have to ask for it back. But, what does respect include? What if we come to the barn when the manager is not present?

Jesus knew He would not stay physically on earth. He knew we needed guidelines that would take us beyond the simple to-do lists of life, and give us guidelines that would answer the deeper questions. He gave us instructions to be in the Word, pray, assemble together and encourage one another (Hebrews 10). Those are the ones we can understand, the simple rules, so to speak. But, He also told us to love Him first, and most of all, and then to love others. He did not say, "Show love to others," although actions are the proof of our love (John 15). He said, "Love your neighbor." He

143

gave an example of His rules by telling the story of the Good Samaritan (Luke 10). An unlikely hero steps in when another man is injured by others and goes beyond the ordinary to make sure the injured one gets better. He goes beyond all expectations for one who will not repay him, for a man he barely knew. He just knew the injured man had needs—and he did what he could to make sure the needs were met.

Barn rules—the easy ones and the complex ones. Godly guidelines are the same. If we keep the simple ones and miss the deep ones, we will find our lives being shallow and empty. We will be safe, but we will not be fulfilled. When we go for deep, when we search for the answers to what is love, respect, holiness—the complexity of a life lived well, doing the hard things in life, even when the Lord is not physically standing in front of us—that is when life takes on true meaning. That's when the rules become a privilege instead of an obligation.

Thought-provoker: Which rules are you keeping? Just the easy ones that have clear expectations, or are you working on the deeper ones that require you trust God to get them?

Lord, we are so easily lured by security and fulfilled expectations. Help us go deeper in our lives to find the true meaning of love and show the world the difference for Your glory.

Amen.

Notes/Insights:

The Water Trough

"Jesus said, 'Everyone who drinks from this water will get thirsty again. But whoever drinks from the water that I will give him will never get thirsty again—ever! In fact, the water I will give him will become a well of water springing up within him for eternal life.'"

John 4:13-14 HCSB

Every morning and evening in the summertime there is a job that needs to be done. The water troughs need to be checked and filled. One hundred gallons does not last long with multiple horses in the dry heat of summer, so the trough gets empty and it needs to be refilled. We fill the buckets and load them on the gator, and then we take the trek out there to fill it up. It is hot, dusty and tiring. Buckets are heavy.

The spring-fed pond, however, does not need to be filled. The bubbly little spring in the bottom of the pond keeps replenishing the water level and makes for a cool, clear drink for the horses whenever they want one. It is a little bit of a walk to the pond for the horses, but it is always there and quenches their thirst.

When Jesus was talking with this woman at the well, He told her His water "…will become a well of water springing up within…." This woman was excited to hear about water she did not have to work to draw. No more heavy buckets, no more heated labor, just water whenever she wanted. A cool, refreshing drink could be hers without all the work.

146

As the encounter with the woman continues, she asks Jesus if He is greater than their father Jacob who gave them the well. The simple answer is, "Yes." He is God and Jacob was not. Jacob had to dig the well; Jesus created the water that was in the well. Jacob lived and died; Jesus is from eternity past to eternity future. Jacob believed God for salvation; Jesus is the Savior.

Jesus teaches this woman a deep spiritual truth—we cannot work for what satisfies our souls. Jesus has provided the soul-refreshing water of salvation and the deep thirst-quenching of a redeemed heart, and we do not get that by working for it. We cannot trudge to the well of the world enough times to get satisfaction. We must turn to the One who gave us life, and know He gives the water of eternal life freely to those who ask Him for it (Acts 16:31). We need to stop trying to fill troughs with water that runs out, and we need to turn to the spring of eternal quenching that we find only in Jesus.

Thought-provoker: What is your thirst today? Will you take the walk to Jesus in faith to find the quenching, the true satisfying answer, to your soul's longing today?

Lord, thank You for all You have provided—especially the spring of living water that comes from You by faith in Your work on Calvary. Help us to find our soul's thirst satisfied in You today.

Amen.

Notes/Insights:

The Winter Storm

"Be merciful to me, O God, be merciful to me, for in you my soul takes refuge; in the shadow of your wings I will take refuge, till the storms of destruction pass by."

Psalm 57:1 ESV

It had been a killer storm—five days of record low temperatures, snow, ice, sleet, freezing rain. Animals had died in the cold, so had eleven people. We prepared for cold, but there is not much that can be done when the temperature is below freezing, and sheets of ice cover roadways and pastures—except keeping the barn doors shut and laying out lots of hay.

When the storms become brutal, there is only one place the horses can go where they will be safe—inside the barn. We close the barn doors. We put blankets on and we lay out hay so they will eat and keep their body temperatures up through the power of digestion. And we keep them in the barn. We don't allow them to go out in the storm—if they wander from the barn they will be covered in ice, chilled by the bitter wind and have a hard time finding something to eat in the frozen pasture. It is better for them to stay in, dry, and as warm as they can be while the storm passes over.

When the bitter storms of life come--when the hope for the future is frozen and we are having a hard time putting one step in front of another, or when the pathways of life are unclear, slick, and dangerous, we need to stay in the barn. We need to stay in the shelter of God's comfort and refuge as He takes the brunt of the storm for us, holds us and keeps our hearts from becoming frozen in the storm. If we try to run from Him, we wind up out in the storm, with no direction, no warmth, no spiritual food. But, when we press into Him, when we refuse to believe He has done something horrible to us, but rather trust that He is taking the brunt of the horrible thing that has just happened, and believe His promises are just as strong and true this moment as they were yesterday, we stay in the barn of His comfort and we will survive the storm.

And the end of this verse tells us that the storm of destruction will pass by. The horses do not have to stay in the barn forever—after the temperature came up and the ice melted away, the horses were able to go back into the pasture and enjoy the safety of the sunshine again. We will feel the warmth of life again, if we stay in the barn of comfort until the storm is passed.

Thought-provoker: What is your habit in the storm? Do you stay in the barn or do you try to go it alone in the cold?

Lord, thank You for the protection of Your mercy and comfort of Your refuge when life is bitter and cold. Help us to stay in the barn when we need to.

Amen.

Notes/Insights:

The Soldier Horse

"My sheep hear My voice, and I know them, and they follow Me."

John 10:27 KJV

His name is Soldado, which means Soldier. He is a light gray, solid, strong horse with a will to match. He protects the herd from outsiders and it takes a long time to gain his trust. Soldado is a great horse, but he knows his job as leader and protector, and he has to keep vigilance in his duty and live up to his name.

Everyone has a hard time with Soldado, except Coy. Coy owns Soldado. Coy is a hard-working teenager and sometimes his work keeps him from coming to see Soldado. But, no matter how long it has been, when Coy shows up, Soldado knows it. All Coy has to do is call to him, and Soldado's demeanor changes. Instead of being a tense protector of the herd, he relaxes. Soldado runs from anyone else, but he comes to Coy. When others have tried to train him, Soldado's strength and strong will have combined to make for a difficult ride. But when Coy rides, Soldado looks like grace in motion. Coy can run Soldado over the hills and through the woods on the farm, and Soldado's grace and strength glisten in the sunlight. When others have seen Soldado as difficult and unyielding, Coy sees a strong horse who needs firm guidance and a gentle hand. He knows how to make the horse move when he doesn't want to and he brings out Soldado's fine qualities. Even when Soldado tests him, Coy's firm, quiet voice assures Soldado that he is not going to win a battle of the wills and it is best for him to submit to Coy's direction and guidance.

Soldado knows Coy's voice. He knows Coy's voice means leadership, trust, dedication and ownership. He knows no matter how long it has been, Coy has not changed. Coy's presence means Soldado can relax and enjoy the time with his owner. Soldado knows challenging Coy will bring a firm, fair hand, a quiet voice and a will stronger than his own. Soldado knows Coy and he is willing to let him lead.

Jesus Christ is the owner. For those who have trusted and accepted His gift of redemption through faith, we belong to Him. We know His voice, and He knows us. He knows how to encourage us, to help us relax and trust, how to discipline us in such a way that we become better. His presence calms us, His voice reassures us, and it makes for a smoother ride.

And though work keeps Coy from coming to see Soldado, Jesus never leaves us (Hebrews 13:5). But, He does not force us to follow Him. We make the choice whether or not to heed His voice. Knowing how much He loves us, it's an easy choice, or at least it should be.

Thought-provoker: Are you listening to the voice of the One who loves you? What is He telling you today through His Word?

Lord, thank You that You know us and Your loving leadership makes us better when we heed Your voice.

Amen.

Notes/Insights:

The Rooster

"Do not love the world or the things in the world. If anyone loves the world, the love of the Father is not in him. For all that is in the world—the desires of the flesh and the desires of the eyes and pride of life—is not from the Father but is from the world."

I John 2:15-16 ESV

There is a beautifully plumed smaller rooster on the farm with our horses. He stands out in the barnyard. He is a bantam rooster with long tail feathers and a crisp red comb. His feathers are gorgeous, bright primary colors mixed with the browns and oranges. When the sun hits his feathers just right, they seem to glow. He is a pretty bird, and that's why it surprised me to find him one day—scratching in the manure pile.

The chickens on the farm are well-fed. Not only are they given chicken scratch, but the horses leave the seedy part of the hay, so the chickens have all of the extra seeds from there, and they can hunt and scratch for insects around the barn and near the pond. There is no lack of nourishment for them. So, why this pretty rooster felt it necessary to be pecking around in the manure pile was beyond my understanding. He had all the wonderful food offered by the farm family, plus the extras left by the horses and yet there he was in the manure. Scratching, pecking, hunting for something that he could not find, he was not satisfied with anything he found in the pile, but he stayed there. I finally could not take it any longer, so I chased him off the

155

pile and back toward the coop where there was fresh water and food waiting for him.

How often do we find ourselves digging around in the world's manure pile for something that will not satisfy our souls? God has provided us with all the nourishment and clean living water we need through His Word, but we find ourselves in the manure pile of life looking for something to satisfy. We are His children, decked out in the beauty of His love, mercy and grace, but instead of standing out, we try to blend into the manure. But, we cannot. Once we have been changed by the redemptive power of God, we stand out. Just like the rooster, our true colors shine when they are hit by the light of God's love. We need to stop looking for worldly desires to satisfy us—they are manure in the barnyard of life. Instead, we need to go back to the nourishment God meant for us to have, then we will find the satisfaction we are hoping for.

Thought-provoker: Are you poking around in the world's manure pile for something? What is it you are looking for, and isn't it far better to find your soul's satisfaction in the purity of God's Word?

Lord, keep us out of the world's manure pile. Help us to remember we can only find our true soul's desire in You.

Amen.

Notes/Insights:

Tank

"Now may the God of peace, who brought up from the dead our Lord Jesus—the great Shepherd of the sheep—with the blood of the everlasting covenant, equip you with all that is good to do His will, working in us what is pleasing in His sight, through Jesus Christ. Glory belongs to Him forever and ever. Amen."

Hebrews 13:20-21 HCSB

Tank is a seventeen hand, beautifully marked, well conformed halter and performance gelding. He has been in the big arenas, won, and even has a display in his breed's museum. He has been shown by well-known individuals and he has brought home every trophy, winner's plate and ribbon one can imagine. His picture has been in the paper and he is the horse that many trainers have desired to have.

One would think a horse like Tank would live in a prestigious trainer's barn with all the amenities money can provide for a horse. He could be living in all the glory of a famous name, or be considered king of the barn. But, he doesn't. Tank lives in the backyard of a teenage girl, Olivia, who is devoted to him, and he is crazy about her. Even in her backyard, his glory as a show horse shines through. Olivia takes him to shows, and he still wins, but his love and devotion is to her and hers to him. Sometimes, they go off on a long trail ride together and enjoy each other's company. When Olivia is upset by something, she goes to Tank to cheer her up. When she is rejoicing about something, she goes to Tank to have him join in the celebration.

Tank is a reminder that the King of Kings and the Lord of Lords, Jesus Christ Himself, chose to lay aside all the splendors of heaven and lay down His life to redeem our hearts. Once resurrected, He could have declared His kingship, taken His kingdom and ruled the world—and one day He will—but in the meantime, He chooses to take up residence, through the Holy Spirit, in the backyard hearts of every person who claims Him as Savior. He does not demand His kingdom in the sense of being revealed to the world at once, but through the lives and actions of those who are His, His glory shines through. Sometimes, He shows His glory in big arenas, and sometimes He takes a trail ride with us as we spend time alone with Him and He reveals Himself to us in more personal ways. When we are upset, or rejoicing, He joins in. The backyard of the hearts of believers is where He wants to live, where He works and where He demonstrates His glory. And we love Him for it.

Thought-provoker: How is your relationship with the King of Kings? Do you realize He has chosen your heart as His dwelling place and He is devoted to you? Live in the reality of this truth today.

Lord, thank You that of all the places in this world, You want to live with us and work through us.

Amen.

Notes/Insights:

The Spoon

"Oil and incense bring joy to the heart, and the sweetness of a friend is better than self-counsel."

Proverbs 27:9 HCSB

A plastic spoon has become a symbol of friendship. One of the dads on our riding team is a comic character fan, and he told the girls about The Tic, an unsung comic hero whose battle cry is, "Spoon!" The girls took up the mantra, and they each carry a spoon at the shows. When standing on the outside of the arena watching another compete, they will yell, "Spoon!" as she passes by on the rail. It's a reminder to relax and enjoy the class, and know that a friend is watching and cheering her on. At one particular show where the atmosphere is more relaxed, two of the girls took the spoons into the arena with them and carried them in their mouths as they rode. When the adults saw what was happening, a burst of laughter came from the stands and the other girls began to cheer. The judge, not knowing what the meaning was, asked about the spoons. The adult assistant in the arena explained the symbol of friendship to the judge and told her about the strong bond between these girls as their friendship carries over into the arena of competition. The judge was impressed that these girls want their friendship to be on display more than their competition. She did judge the class based on the criteria of horse and rider, but she went away with a picture of friendship that will hopefully bring a smile to her face every time she sees a plastic spoon.

A plastic spoon, a simple utensil that represented so much more in the lives of these girls and their families. The sweetness of friendship among competitors—what a concept for the children of God to embrace. In this competitive, ladder-climbing, me-first culture, we can stand out, not because of our aggressive attitude, but because of our friendship. We can be the spoon-carriers who cheer each other on and help each other succeed. Philippians 2 tells us that we are to look after the welfare of each other. So many times we make life an "every man for himself" mentally. We see a weakness in another, and we exploit it to our advantage. We take the opportunity to get ahead—but get ahead where? What direction are we headed that it is better to go alone than to journey together? Let's put down the sledge hammer of competition and let's pick up a spoon. In life, we are all in this together. It is not the world's philosophy, but God's principle is that we are better as we help others. We become successful as we journey in friendship with others and we ride together. Now, where is that plastic spoon?

Thought-provoker: Do you have "spoon" friendships in your life? Who are those who help you become better by their friendship? Whom do you make better with yours?

Lord, thank You for friendships. Help us to remember Your way of life is so different from the world.

Amen.

Notes/Insights:

The Cacklers

"Or what woman, who has ten silver coins, if she loses one coin, does not light a lamp, sweep the house, and search carefully until she finds it? When she finds it, she calls her women friends and neighbors together, saying, 'Rejoice with me, because I have found the silver coin I lost!' I tell you, in the same way, there is joy in the presence of God's angels over one sinner who repents."

Luke 15:8-10 HCSB

There are many interesting things to learn on a farm. I am learning a lot about chickens. There are ten chickens that live on the farm with the horses and I am being taught how to care for them, how to gather eggs, and how to recognize different chicken characteristics. I have learned how to tell the different chickens apart, by markings and temperaments and I have fun watching the roosters strut about and show off their plumes. I have learned that there are three types of chickens on the farm, and each breed has their distinctions, but they all stay together for safety and companionship. One of the things I have had to get used to is the cackling. Whenever a hen gets ready to lay an egg, she starts to cackle and lets everyone know about the happy event. She is preparing for a new life, an egg that she will set on, protect and nurture until it is hatched.

When one starts, all the other hens join in. They spread the word that an egg is being laid and they seem to be happy for the egg layer. They continue to cackle and call until all the other hens have heard and join in the noise. No one is left out, and it can get quite loud in the coop during the whole process, as each hen has her own way of spreading the news.

Wouldn't it be interesting if all of us decided to join in and spread the word every time a new believer was added to the kingdom? What if we all joined in the celebration, much like the hens do over a new egg, and we made such a happy fuss that others would wonder what we were up to? The passage tells us that there is joy in heaven over one sinner that repents. With all the rejoicing that goes on in heaven, we should want to join in down here. We are all different, and we rejoice in different ways, but we should celebrate so others see the joy about the wonderful event of a new birth (John 3:3), and we should be happy to spread the news. It's time to start celebrating.

Thought-provoker: Do you rejoice when you hear of others who have joined God's family? How do you rejoice? Do others see your rejoicing?

Lord, thank You for the privilege to be a part of the rejoicing when one enters Your kingdom. Help us to celebrate loudly enough that our joy spills over and causes others to join in.

Amen.

Notes/Insights:

The Farrier

"According to God's grace that was given to me, I have laid a foundation as a skilled master builder, and another builds on it. But each one must be careful how he builds on it. For no one can lay any other foundation than what has been laid down. That foundation is Jesus Christ."

I Corinthians 3:10-11 HCSB

Our farrier is a very important part of our horse journey. Without him, our horses would not have the foundation of good shoes and their gaits would be hindered or halted. Barry has gone to school to learn how to shod the horses correctly and he knows how to prevent issues with proper shoeing. He has studied the conformation and gaits of different breeds and he takes his time as he set each shoe. We do not trust just anyone to throw shoes on our horses and get riding. If one of the horses does throw a shoe, we wait for Barry to come and replace it because we know he will do the job correctly and take care of the problem.

In addition to being a good farrier, Barry is a good man. He is patient with the different horses. As he shoes our horses, he talks with our daughter to find out what her plans are for the coming weeks with her horse Dancer, what type of riding they are going to be doing, and he makes recommendations about changes we should make in shoe material or size to maximize the training benefits. He truly cares about the horses and riders and he makes the farrier visit a good experience for both. If there is a tough decision to be made, if there is an injury that requires rest from

167

training or something that needs to be changed so the horse stays sound, Barry stands firm on the truth and guides us through the process to help us find the right solution.

Barry is a good example of what a teacher should be. He has studied and learned the materials, and his training goes deep. He then shares his knowledge with others, setting a good foundation. He listens and works with the horses and riders to maximize their training and to help them avoid problems. And when tough decisions need to be made, when the truth needs to be shared for the welfare of the horse and rider, Barry does not back down or keep silent. Teachers need to be willing to do this as well, for there are tough truths in the Word that others need to hear. We cannot change the foundation just because others do not want to hear it. Teachers need to remember others trust their guidance and their discernment, just as we trust Barry, and they need to be careful how they build on the foundation of Jesus Christ. Being a farrier, or a teacher, is a big responsibility. We are glad ours is a good one.

Thought-provoker: Are you listening to good Godly teachers? Are you teaching truth, even when it is tough?

Lord, thank You that You are the foundation. Help us be careful how we build.

Amen.

Notes/Insights:

The Twins

"And not only that, but we also rejoice in our afflictions, because
we know that affliction produces endurance, endurance produces
proven character, and proven character produces hope."

Romans 5:3-4 HSCB

Anna and Cara are identical twins who love horses and are
committed team members in our Hippology program. They
are good students, and they are also quiet and respectful in
the classroom. I did not realize their tenacity and
perseverance until I had the privilege to see them ride. Anna
and Cara love to ride hunter jumpers. While watching them
at practice, they would take their horses in the arena, get
them up to a canter and then guide them to the jumps. I
caught my breath as one of the twins guided her horse
toward the jump at a full canter, and just as she posted to
make the jump, he refused. He stopped dead in his tracks,
which meant she went over the top and landed hard. She
got right back up, dusted off her backside, remounted and
started the pattern again. Twice he refused, but the third
time, she pushed him over and he sailed over the fence. The
smile when they landed was priceless. She trotted him
around the arena and then went back to the line to wait her
next turn. She was not going to give up on this event that
she loved so much, and she knew the horse had the ability
to do well. As she waited in line, she talked with her sister
and though I could not hear the words, I could see the
encouragement. There was hope that the next time he

would do the jump correctly the first time, no refusals, and their training would be worth it.

The twins endure. They endure bumps and bruises when they fall. They endure stubbornness from their horses as they work to train them to accept the jumps and learn to compete. They endure the discomfort of a failed jump; they endure the embarrassment that sometimes comes when their horses refuse what they know they should do. And their endurance has paid off—they are becoming very good riders and they are succeeding in their events. They have the hope of better days ahead, and they encourage each other to keep on going.

The Christian walk is peppered with afflictions that produce endurance. When we endure, our character deepens and that depth produces hope. Hope for better days ahead, and the knowledge that walking away is not an option. We will smile again, and the bumps and bruises make the success that much sweeter. Find your twin—the one to encourage you—and hang in there. We have hope.

Thought-provoker: What are you enduring that will deepen your character? Are you encouraging others when you see their struggles? Are you offering hope?

Lord, thank You for the hope we have in You. Thank You that endurance builds character and character recognizes hope. Help us endure and encourage others to do the same.

Amen.

Notes/Insights:

The Guardian

"O Timothy! Guard what was committed to your trust, avoiding the profane and idle babblings and contradictions of what is falsely called knowledge—by professing it some have strayed concerning the faith."

I Timothy 6:20-21 NKJV

He stands in the pasture, black as midnight against the blonde hay around him. He watches over the young ones, the older mares and the playful geldings. He stands away from the herd, keeping a watchful eye. He is wise, older, and mature. He does not get involved in the skirmishes between mares over hay flakes or the water trough. He does not participate in the endless, pointless battles between the geldings. He leads the herd in for shelter at night, and he waits for them to turn out in the mornings. He stays calm and steady. His name is Shaker and he is the guardian.

Shaker is a good example of a guardian. He knows what to watch for—he knows who the enemies of the herd are and he keeps a watchful eye to make sure they do not invade the pasture. He takes his responsibility to guard as a trust that was committed to him by the owners of the farm, and though it is an innate instinct, he does not stray from the duty he has. He does not decide to run off alone somewhere for the day and forget to keep watch. He is faithful.

We, as Christians, are called to be guardians. In the passage today, we are reminded that the Gospel and the truth of God's Word were committed to our trust. We are to be faithful in guarding that truth, and we are not to be sucked into pointless arguments about the profane, or listen to idle babblings that contradict God's Word. Even if others call it "knowledge," or "enlightenment," if it is contrary to Scripture it needs to be discarded. Accepting or professing something other than the truth can cause us to stray from the faith. We do not want anything to draw us away from the faith—what keeps that from happening? Being a guardian of the truth, just as Shaker is in the pasture. How do we accomplish this? Paul tells Timothy in his second letter that the way to stay faithful to the truth is to study the Word (2 Timothy 2:15). The more we know of the truth, the more likely we are to see contradictions with the world's philosophy (2 Timothy 3:16-17). When we guard the truth, the world's lies—even what is called knowledge—are exposed for what they are, enemies that can hurt the herd and cause others to stray. When we immerse ourselves in the truth, deception is easier to spot—and to avoid.

Thought-provoker: What steps are you taking to guard the truth in your own life and spot deception?

Lord, thank You for the truth that protects us. Help us to guard the truth so You can show us the deception and error that will lead us astray. Then, turn us back to the truth so that does not happen. Thank You.

Amen.

Notes/Insights:

The Gift Horse

"Thanks be to God for His indescribable gift!"

2 Corinthians 9:15 NKJV

Almost a year after the accident, I met a horse named Julio. A friend invited us to come and ride with them at their farm, and she had chosen Julio for me that day. I enjoyed the day riding with friends, and Julio seemed to enjoy it as well.

That day was a divine appointment. A few weeks later, we moved our horse Dancer and her buddy, Shaker, to that farm. The friend who had asked me to ride was Marsha, the one who owns the farm with her husband, Rod, and the farm family who has taken us in as part of their own. Rod and Marsha allowed me to continue to ride Julio through the fall and they spent time helping me learn how to ride the Paso Fino style.

What I did not know until later, was that Julio's former rider had passed away and he had been stand-offish with others since that had happened. I had spent the summer gaining back my confidence as a rider after the accident and the sale. I had borrowed the spotted saddle horse my friend had generously offered, and I was getting back to being at ease in the saddle. Julio seemed to sense that I needed him to continue that progress, and we connected.

We rode through the fall—a mild season had allowed us to extend our riding into late November. Rod and Marsha allowed me to ride Julio and they noticed my confidence continuing to grow and his demeanor beginning to change in a good way. I was content to know I was improving as a rider, and I was happy to have such a sweet horse to enjoy through the season.

Christmas came—one of my favorite times of the year. Gifts, lights, the Gospel being spelled out through manger scenes and Christmas carols, I enjoyed every moment. The last gift of the season was from my husband. After all the hustle and bustle of the holidays, we were in the living room and he handed me an envelope. Inside were the ownership papers for Julio—my husband had bought me the horse that I had come to love and dream about. John's love and generosity had seen the bond between me and Julio and he decided to bless me with this gift. My joy overflowed as I went to the farm to see him and to be able to call him "mine."

God's gift was Himself. And as much as I love Julio, I love my husband so much more as the gift-giver. God knew what we needed was more than confidence, borrowed lives and the search for contentment and joy. We needed Him—to be called His own and to know the love of a lifetime that overcomes any obstacle and overflows with the greatest joy. So, He gave.

Thought-provoker: Have you ever stopped to think about the greatest gift being God Himself? How have you accepted His gift?

Lord, thank You for the indescribable gift—the giving of Yourself so You could call us Yours. Remind us to live in the love and joy today.

Amen.

Notes/Insights:

The Silhouette

"Pursue righteousness, godliness, faith, love, steadfastness, gentleness. Fight the good fight of the faith. Take hold of the eternal life to which you were called and about which you made the good confession in the presence of many witnesses."

I Timothy 6:11b-12 ESV

At the end of every good Western or horse movie, there is a silhouette of the horse and rider going off into the sunset. Sometimes, the hero and heroine go together, sometimes, it's just one. They head off to the next adventure and the theme music lets the audience know that all has ended well and everything will be okay in the coming days.

As we close this journey through horse country, we have learned many things together: perseverance, hope, joy, faith, humility, encouragement, steadfastness. We have looked at many different aspects of horse-loving and farm-living, and we have made it to the end of this particular trail. But the ride is not over. There is so much more for each of us to do, and as good heroes and heroines, we follow the trail to new beginnings and we find the next adventure the Lord has for us. We take the lessons we have learned with us, and we tuck away the treasures of this journey in our heart trailer as we move on. We remember the good things that have made us better; we remind ourselves of the lessons we have learned to leave bitterness behind, celebrate the love of God in our lives and others, and give forgiveness where we should. We recall the great love of God and how He has promised to journey with us through this life, and the promise of forever with Him when this trail is ended.

So, we continue to ride. We continue to make a good confession in the presence of many witnesses—we let others know how good God is and how His redemption has changed our hearts forever. We can continue to go forward because we know He holds the future where we are headed, and it will be a good journey. We know to flee the things that will make the ride rough and hard, and we take hold of the promises that God has given that make the ride worth it, no matter if we go over mountains or through the valleys. Through tough days of training, days of joy and success, winter storms, and moments of victory, we know He is with us. That is what makes the journey worthwhile. Enjoy the ride.

Thought-provoker: As this ride comes to an end, please take a few moments to meditate on the lessons you have learned and what God wants you to take away from this journey. May you find you are different for the time you have invested, and you are loved.

Lord, thank You for the final step of this journey, but thank You that our ride is not over until we have our forever with You. As we go forward, help us to remember what You have taught us, and help us to enjoy the ride.

Amen.

Notes/Insights:

About the Author

Tammy Chandler is a wife, mother, teacher, friend, author and public speaker. She accepted Christ as Savior when she was five years old, dedicated her life to full-time service as a teenager and has worked in various ministries for the past twenty years. She has a bachelor of education degree from Clearwater Christian College, and a master of education degree from Jones International University. After many year of using everyday objects to teach children and teenagers, God allowed her to write Devotions from Everyday Things (Westbow Press), its follow-up, More Devotions from Everyday Things and Devotions from Everyday Things: Horse and Farm Edition, to include a larger audience.

When she is not writing, Tammy enjoys spending time with her husband, John, watching their teenage sons play sports, going horseback riding with their daughter, or playing fetch with their dog, Ava. The Chandlers live in Tennessee.

Visit Tammy online at:

www.simplydevotions.wordpress.com

You might also enjoy these fine books from:

WordCrafts Press

ProVerb Ponderings
> (31 Ruminations on Positive Action)
> by Rodney Boyd

Morning Mist
> (Stories from the Water's Edge)
> by Barbie Loflin

Why I Failed in the Music Business
> (and how NOT to follow in my footsteps)
> by Steve Grossman

Youth Ministry is Easy!
> (and 9 other lies)
> by Aaron Shaver

Chronicles of a Believer
> by Don McCain

Illuminations
> by Paula K. Parker & Tracy Sugg

www.wordcrafts.net